Twitter Super-Charged

How to Make Twitter Work for You

Dr Earl R Smith II

Published by Raven Press

DrSmith@Dr-Smith.com
www.Dr-Smith.com

I0483127

Raven Press

About Dr. Smith

I provide mentoring to those who have both the courage and determination to make a truly transformational journey. My approach is heavily influenced by core principles of Zen Buddhism. I don't offer quick fixes or follow the latest fads. If you are willing to make the long journey – if it's time for you to come to know the person you really are and can become – if you intend to finally find the path you should be following – if you want to start living life you were truly meant to live – then perhaps we should talk.

Other Books by Dr. Smith

- Zen Mentoring – Forty Meditations
- The CEO's Handbook - Volume One: Forty-Six Meditations for a Thinking Chief Executive
- The CEO's Handbook Volume Two Business Development
- The CEO's Handbook - Volume Three Getting Funded by Angel Investors
- The CEO's Handbook Volume Four - The Money Chase
- Understanding Venture Capital
- Leadership - Notes From a Successful Entrepreneur and Experienced Coach
- Dream Walk - Parables for the Living

~~~~~~

Table of Contents

Monetizing Twitter

- Creating a Target Audience
- Monetizing Twitter by Utilizing Keywords
- Product Promotion and Affiliate Links on Twitter
- Tools that Will Make Your Twitter Feed Shine
- Techniques to Avoid When Monetizing Social Media
- Why Your Business Should Use Promoted Accounts on Twitter
- Introduce a Business to Twitter with Promoted Tweets
- Getting Your Tweets to Fly - How to Successfully Promote Your Twitter Business Account
- Twitter Promotion and How it Can Help Your Business to Soar
- Trending Tweets - Why Your Business Should Seek to Reach the Top
- Why Promoted Trends Can Help Businesses To Improve their Twitter Ranking

Summing Up

Introduction

I've written this book after years of using Twitter. I've made lots of mistakes along the way and watched other do the same. Sure, there were some successes but, for the most part, I didn't like the results I was seeing for my time and efforts. There came a time when I was ready to give up on the whole thing. I wasn't seeing any significant return from the time and energy that was going into using Twitter. It seemed like a colossal waste.

Then something happened that began to turn my experience around. I decided to give it one more shot and began to experiment with different ways of using Twitter. I asked some of my Twitter connections about their approach to Tweeting. I read anything and everything I could find on how to make Twitter work – how to make it pay off. Over time, a new approach to using Twitter emerged. My purpose in writing this book is to help you learn from my mistakes and to help you avoid them. But more than that, I want to help you get real benefits out of your participation in one of the most useful social media platforms available.

Twitter is one of the most powerful social media platforms. Or at least it can be. Most people never come close to unlocking the incredible power that it offers. I will show you how to break away from the crowd and join that tiny group of Twitter users who are achieving truly amazing results. You can be stunningly successful – a creative Twitter genius. And the real secret is that it's not rocket science. It's just a matter of understanding how Twitter works and transforming the way you use Twitter – adopting a dynamic, inventive and powerful approach.

This book will show you how to revolutionize your Twitter experience. It will show you how to make meaningful changes to the way you currently use Twitter. The results will be a metamorphosis from an unproductive experience to a genuinely impressive systematic approach. You will begin to see a positive return on the time and energy you spend. You are not the first to learn of this approach. I have schooled others on what I have learned – passed around drafts of this book. Here are some comments from those people:

"As an author, I've read numerous books on how to market my novels, but none of them was very helpful. They either gave information that was too broad or promoted the idea of a cyberspace door-to-door salesman. While Dr. Smith's book is not specifically about marketing, it teaches the proper method to use twitter so that you can market without offending or annoying. Dr. Smith gave many useful tips and examples throughout the book that any novice can find helpful. I now feel more confident about my marketing efforts and am ready to jump in to twitter!"

"This book is a very practical guide to using Twitter as a marketing tool and how to get the most from Twitter. Its suggestions on building followers, engaging in conversations and being a good Twitter citizen have proven invaluable to me. I have used it as a road map to build my brand while extending my reach.

This book has allowed me to promote my advisory practice in a very professional way that generates goodwill and interest in my services. I would recommend this guide for anyone that wants to build their brand, promote their practice or to generate interesting, intelligent conversations with like-minded people."

"This book is a brilliant and highly useful description of how to turn Twitter into an excellent marketing and branding instrument. Every chapter has hints that helped me improve the return on my efforts. I refer to the book constantly. It is a

remarkable resource. I urge you to publish it."

"I couldn't believe how badly I was at using Twitter until I read your book. But you went beyond showing me how I was messing up; you showed me how to become a Twitter star. I am ever grateful to you for that."

"Reading this book and then applying your ideas has been an exhilarating experience. I thought that I knew how to use Twitter but I realize that I was just an amateur. Now my Twitter accounts have become a major part of my branding and marketing efforts. The results have been stunning."

"I can't thank you enough for this book. The skillful way you open opportunities for improvement has made it easy to gain mastery. I now have a thriving, robust and systematic approach to using Twitter. It has opened exciting possibilities and a virtually limitless range of possibilities."

"I must admit that, before I read your book, I had taken a very casual approach to Twitter and was getting very little out of it. The book has revolutionized my approach. The change is remarkable. Now I am a Twitter fan big time."

"Each chapter brought new and powerful ideas. The book is easy to read – deceptively so given the eye-opening tidbits that seem to flow one after another. I've always believed that knowledge is power. This book has made me a more skillful and powerful Twitter user."

"This remarkable book has helped me visualize an entirely new approach to using Twitter. Each chapter is full of *solutions that increase my abilities to generate real benefits from Twitter. The language is strong and direct – easy to read and understand. Some of the nuggets are truly mind-blowing. Thank you for this unique and highly valuable book."*

"I never suspected how powerful a 140 character message could be until I started applying the lessons in your book. Now I spend less time on Twitter and am getting benefits galore. Thanks for a great book."

"I would never have believed it. I've gotten new business and new friends from Twitter. If you had told me a few months back that both would happen, I would have laughed in your face. You showed me the way and I am forever grateful. Thanks, Doc."

How to Use This Book

You will find useful nuggets in every chapter – at least this was my hope as I wrote this book. After you've read it all the way through, you might want to go back to individual chapters and select one or two strategies to try out. I suspect that you will find the process of improving your Twitter experience will go better that way rather than if you try them all out at once. Remember, you are working to change habits that may have grown over months or years. Like Rome, a good Twitter presence is not built in a day. It takes developing good skills and then turning them into habits. And, as the saying goes, can take weeks before a new behavior becomes a habit.

Branding, Nuggets and Meadow Muffins

Your Account is Your Brand

Twitter is a social media platform with immense possibilities and power. It allows you to connect with thousands of people and companies through a simple 140 character message called a Tweet. It is very easy to use. In fact, its ease of entry is one of the reasons that most people get it wrong. The biggest problem that most people have with social media platforms like Twitter is that it seems intuitive; easy to use. They establish an account and begin twittering away. And that's when the problems begin to accumulate.

Twitter can be addictive and the addiction often starts with the first Tweet. Some people fall into a casual approach to Tweeting because they haven't thought through the why or how of using social media. By that I don't mean the why or how to use social media. I mean the why and how of their use of Twitter. It's not a question of how to use Twitter but of why you use Twitter. Without the 'why' the 'how' can be lead to a real waste of time. People who fail to think the 'why' question through don't carefully reflect on questions such as:

- Why do I want to spend time and effort using Twitter?
- What do I expect to get out of being a Twitter user?
- How can I realize benefits from the time I spend Tweeting?
- What 'brand' do I want to promote – my personal brand, a company brand, a social brand, a professional brand?

These and many more questions have a common focus – Twitter means that you are establishing a brand through your Tweets. You should clearly understand what you intend that brand to stand for and how it will help you achieve your goals. Not addressing these questions is much like getting in a car and just driving. Driving without a destination in mind may be pleasant for a while but most humans prefer to be driving somewhere and for some purpose. So, the question with Twitter usage is where to and why?

Let's start with the idea of establishing a brand. Suppose that you have an interest' dog training. You might want to become known in the Twitterverse as an expert in the area. Establishing that brand would lead other users to seek you out. Perhaps you would gain customers for your business or new knowledge to help you become a better dog trainer. Twitter can help you do that.

But there is more to Twitter. Let's say that you want to build a network of other people who are also interested in dog training. Twitter can help you build the network faster than any other social media platform. In a very short time, you could have hundreds – or maybe thousands - of followers also interested in training dogs. A list of followers, correctly constructed, is one the most valuable assets that Twitter can help you build. Your followers would be a regular source of ideas. You could engage some of them in extended conversations about this or that aspect of dog training. Exchanging ideas with people with similar interests is one of the things that Twitter facilitates best. Your home feed is regularly restocked with fresh Tweets from the people you are following. Every Tweet is an invitation to a potential conversation. And it goes on twenty-four hours a day, seven days a week!

Then there are the people you would follow. You could build and expand a list people who regularly Tweet high quality information on dog training and related topics such as dog health, breed information, supplies, food and much more. Twitter allows you to do searches for these people and helps you connect with them. Many that you follow will follow you back, increasing your list of followers.

It's Cumulative

One of the best things about Twitter is that it is cumulative. By that I mean that your list of followers and those you follow grows over time. One of the principal focuses of this book – particularly in this section – is to show you how to build those lists in a way that yields maximum benefits. At the end of a year using Twitter the right way, you will probably have thousands of followers and be following thousands more. The longer you use Twitter, the longer your lists will grow.

But there is another, far more important way that Twitter is cumulative and that is the true focus of this book. Twitter allows you to establish a brand that gets more widely recognized with every passing day – that is if you approach Tweeting in the right way. Of course, there is always the opposite possibility. If you are sloppy about defining and establishing your brand you can end up as just so much background noise in the Twitterverse.

If you first think through the brand that you want to establish and then set about purposefully both establishing it and building a community of users around it, Twitter is one of the most powerful social media platforms available. So the first step is defining that brand. Before you set about sending your first Tweet, it is a good idea to decide just who you are going to be on Twitter. Now, I can hear you asking, "What do you mean, who I am going to be? I am me!" Sure, but remember that that your brand is going to be communicated via a series of 140 character Tweets to people who mostly don't know you, will probably never meet you and have none of the context of "I am me."

Twitter users generally fall into two broad categories. The first is what I call the great and general diffusion. When you come across their accounts, it's hard to tell who they are or what their interests are. In the second category, there are those who have decided who they are going to be on Twitter and are taking the time and making the effort to communicate that to people who might be interested in following them. The best users – the most successful ones – know precisely who they intend to be on Twitter, what they want to accomplish by Tweeting and how to tell whether their time and efforts are paying off.

Twelve Strategies to Build Strong Following & Follower Bases

At the heart of any effective Twitter strategy are the two great pillars of followers and followed. The people you follow are the ones who are going to contribute to your own home feed. It is important that you carefully select followers who are going to be regularly Tweeting things that you are interested in. The people who follow you are going to see your Tweets on their home feed. In short, you want people to follow you who bring you value through their tweets and followers who will value your contribution and pass them on to their followers.

This last idea is worth a closer glance. If you have followers who find your Tweets interesting, they can Retweet them to their followers. A single follower, who might have say five thousand followers, would pass on your Tweet to all them by Retweeting. Maybe three or four of those followers might further pass on your Tweet. Say they had a few thousand each. It does not take long to get your Tweet before many thousands of users. This multiplier effect is one of the most potent reasons for Tweeting.

At this point, and before the drool starts to run down your chin, it is important to go back to the point I made about numbers for numbers sake. If your Tweets get passed on to a million users; all of whom have no interest in what you have written, what's the point?

The very same dynamic rules when you look at your list of people you follow. You will see their Tweets in your home feed. That's how the bulk of your feed is generated. Say your interest is in dog training. If you have carefully built the list of people you follow, most of them will also be interested in dog training. As a result, most of the Tweets in your home field will touch, in one way or another, on that topic. If you build that list right, you will have established a community of people with a common interest. That community is a potent asset. It gives you a deep and reliable resource of information, connections and a constant flow of ideas about dog training.

So, how do you build that very valuable asset and how to you keep if from turning into a useless, fetid swamp of irrelevancies, hookers, halfwits and scammers? Well, here are a few suggestions:

Start with a vision

Twitter is so easy to begin to use that most people skip the essential first questions. Here are just a few that you should ask before you begin Tweeting:

- What do you want to get out of participating?
- What interests do you want to pursue?
- Who should you be connecting with (followers)?
- Who do you want to connect with you (following)?
- What are your principal goals in using Twitter?
- How will you measure the results of your time and effort against your goals?

Answering these questions will allow you to take a coherent and focused approach to Twitter. People with a well thought-out plan will always receive benefits that the unprepared would never conceive of. If you take the time to think through why you are going to get involved in Twitter, what you expect in return, how you will know if your expectations are being met and if the effort is paying off, you will be head and shoulders above the vast majority of users.

Post quality content

In Twitter, content is king. And the king of kings of content is interesting, useful information that is not a sales pitch and invites responses. In other words, the best Tweets are ones which get conversations going. And one measure of how well you are doing using Twitter is how often your Tweets are responded too. Are you just sending them out into the void and never hearing back from people who encounter them? If so, what is the point of spending all that time and effort? Sure, you may make some sales of whatever thing you are selling but Twitter is a pretty inefficient way to sell anything. And that's not the point of social media anyway. It will take some practice but eventually you will get the knack of Tweeting in a way that induces responses. At that point you will open a potential that you never expected. Your network will begin to come alive and engage with you. Quality content elicits quality responses. You will learn from others. But first, you have to prime the pump and prove that you are worth engaging with.

Align your Tweets with your interests

If you have done the heavy lifting of the first step and committed to posting quality content, the next stop along the way is to make sure that you are posting Tweets that align with your interests. This is important for a range of reasons. The first is that it reinforces the branding that you are working to establish. If your Tweets are all over the lot, people will see you as being unfocused and uninteresting. Remember, you are not trying to be interesting to everybody – only the people you find interesting. If your Tweets are closely related on the interests listed in your profile, other

16

users will see you as focused.

A second reason is that focused Tweets will attract the kinds of followers that you want. They will engage with you and decide to follow you because their interests align with yours.

A third reason is that you will be delivering value both to the people who follow you and to potential followers. In addition, you will be delivering value to people you follow. They will visit your website and see your Tweets. They will begin to retweet them or favorite them. Remember, its social media! Focused Tweets will help you build a high-quality following that you can go to and receive useful information from. Remember, such a following is a major asset when you need information or contacts that might advance your interests. The good rule is know yourself and then be yourself.

Respond to quality

You should always spend time reading the Tweets in your home feed. I am amazed at how little time most Twitter users spend doing this. There are several reasons why it's a very good idea. The most important one is that you will see what the people you follow are Tweeting. You will identify those Tweets that are particularly helpful or interesting. Let's say you are building a following around gardening and one of the people you follow Tweets something that turns on all sorts of lights between your ears. What do you do? Well, first, of course, you take in the information. But what then? Well, you might reply to their Tweet – thanking them for the information and letting them know how much you enjoyed reading it. This is the beginning of a conversation and might lead to other gems. Second, you might Retweet or Favorite their Tweet. That would send it on to all your followers with your mark of approval. Most users will see that as a compliment and many will respond by Retweeting one of your Tweets.

17

The basic reason to respond to quality is that quality Tweets indicate users who you might gain much from engaging with. These are the very people you have been looking to connect with. Now that you have found them, connect!

Retweet quality

As you run down your home feed, you'll some across Tweets that you find particularly interesting and that you suspect your followers will find interesting as well. Twitter makes it very easy to share Tweets. If you hover your cursor overt the areas just below each Tweet, you will see a menu appear. It allows you to reply, retweet, favorite, share by email, embed or report the Tweet. Retweeting is your way of telling someone you follow that their Tweet is worth sending on to your followers. It is your way of saying, "I think that my followers should see this!" There is an unwritten rule in Twitter. If you would be Retweeted, Retweet in return. But, before your go crazy with the Retweet option, remember that people who Retweet crap are seen as ... Well, you get the picture, I'm sure.

Favorite quality

If you find a Tweet that is particularly good, you have another option. Let's say that it's not one that you want to send on to your followers – perhaps it is off topic for your branding purposes – but you found it useful. You can 'Favorite' the Tweet. This tells the Tweeter that they posted something that you found interesting, useful or just pleasantly distracting. It's a way to send a compliment.

Screen those you chose to follow

There is a great temptation to follow everybody but, in Twitter terms, that makes you nobody. Remember, the key to getting the most out of Twitter is coherent branding. You are known, to a great extent, by who it is that you associate with. People who are deciding whether to follow you will often review your list of followers. You might think that is not the case but you do so at your peril. I regularly conduct such a screening and never connect with users who had a follow list full of hookers, halfwits and scammers. A second reason why you benefit from carefully choosing who to follow is that you will develop a much more valuable asset – a regular source of high-quality Tweets on subjects that you are interested in. With Twitter, your list of followers and those who you follow are the two most important assets you develop – they are the principal returns for the time you spend Tweeting. Who you follow determines how valuable to you your home feed will become. If you choose carefully, you will have a home feed that you can't wait to read.

Screen those who follow you

As your number of followers increases, you will get an increasing number of users who want to follow you. At something around ten thousand followers, the hookers, halfwits and scammers start to try to join your followers list. Twitter has a very useful tool for dealing with these barnacles that are looking to attach to the hull of your Twitter sloop. It's called 'Blocking'.

Let's say that you go to your list of followers and discover that you now have people who are following you but you are not following. There are users who have discovered your Tweets or found you through a search. For one reason or another, they have decided to follow you. Now you have a choice to make. You can either follow them back, decide not to follow them or block them. The first one is easy. You click on their user name and visit their profile page. You take a look at their Tweets, followers and those they follow. If the last two are lists full of people you might find interesting, you click on the 'Follow' button.

If your research does not leave you interested but the user is benign, you may just do nothing. Most likely, they will unfollow you after some time.

The third option is your chance to help keep the streets and alleys of Twitter clean. You can 'Block' them. This tells the user that they a can no longer connect with your account. You can also block and then report the user for spam. These are options that I use on a regular basis. Twitter is fertile ground for hookers, halfwits, spammers and scammers. I like to do my part when it comes to taking out the trash.

Make Lists

Twitter has a highly useful option that allows you to organize the most important of your followers into lists. If you click on the down arrow to the left of the Follow button next to the name of someone you follow, one of the options is to add or remove the user to a list. You can keep all sorts of lists and sort your contacts by a whole range of criteria. You can then target Tweets and Replies, Favorite, Retweet and more. It is highly a useful capability that I urge you to explore. You can make your lists either private or public. If you make them public, others can subscribe to the list and follow it. If it is a private list, only you can see the feed from it. Most experienced Twitter users maintain an extensive collection of both private and public lists.

Engage in conversations

I know, I've said it before. Twitter is a social media site. It's all about finding people who share your interests and engaging them in conversations about those interests. Compared to other, less effective uses like selling something or proselytizing, this is the tenderloin of Twitter – the sweet spot – its *raison d'etre*. Nothing that you get out of using Twitter will compare in value. Nothing will better allow you to monetize your time and effort. In a Twitterverse that sometimes seems to be populated with people standing on soapboxes and yelling into the void, it's the conversations that are yielding real value. I regularly scan down my home feed to find opportunities to open conversations. If you try it, you will be surprised at how willing - indeed eager – some Twitter users are to engage in discussions. And remember to add good conversational partners to a list!

Keep your home feed clean

I regularly scan my home feed for trash. No matter how hard you work to screen out hookers, halfwits and scammers, some are going to slip through. Some are lurking behind disguises and then show their true colors. Others Tweet something of substance and then launch in to proselytizing or their snake oil routines. The bad pennies, I block and unfollow. Remember, your home feed, along with your followers and the list of those you follow, are you front door and front and back yards. They are the highly visible indicators of what kind of a neighbor you will be. Tend to them carefully.

Multitask

A final suggestion that you may find helpful is how to implement many of the suggestions above efficiently and effectively. Whenever I am reading my home feed, I am applying several screens at once. I am looking for interesting Tweets to respond to. I am also monitoring ongoing conversations. If there are barnacles, I scrape them off. I regularly Favorite and Retweet Tweets when warranted. I am also on the hunt for interesting conversations between other users that I can join in on.

The same is true when I am looking at people to follow. If I visit their list of followers, I may Retweet something or Favorite a Tweet. I would certainly block someone that I don't want to end up on my home feed. (Think of it as a prophylactic strike) I take notice of users whose list of followers is particularly interesting to me and add those users to one of my lists.

The message is that, the better you get at multitasking the more you will get done and the better return you will realize on your time and effort.

Summary

The dozen suggestions above are only the beginning of learning how to get the most out of your Twitter experience. The more thought you put into it, the more ways you will come up with to increase the value of your experience. Don't stagnate. Think, learn, experiment, change, grow and reap the harvest of your efforts.

Twenty-One Self-Sabotaging Ways to Appear Inept on Twitter

When deciding how to participate in a social media forum like Twitter, it is important to understand the way it works and how your actions will impact your experience - and the benefits you get from the time you spend. One important way that you can do that is to view your participation through the eyes of those who will be looking at you as a potential connection.

The first thing that you need to come to terms with is the incredibly short time that you have to make a positive enough first impression to induce those who you will value being connected with to take the step of clicking the 'Follow' button. All users have their own way of deciding when to click that button but they all have one thing in common. Users most often make the decision of whether or not to follow someone in seconds, meaning that you have very little time to impress.

As I mentioned in the introduction, this book was written for those who want to take a serious and balanced approach to Twitter; users who are more interested in what they get for their time spent and what they can contribute in return. For them, the list below should serve as a 'don't go there' set of guidelines.

Let's Start With Your Profile

When you first started using Twitter, you probably didn't spend much time thinking about your profile. You probably just winged it. You were you describing you to yourself. But it's a good idea to take a look at how other people will see your Twitter profile and from their perspective. Imagine a finger poised above that 'Follow' button as a user reads your profile. In seconds they decide to either move on or click the button.

How does this momentous situation develop? Generally it comes about in one of four ways. First, someone may find you in his or her home stream. Twitter helps you find people you might want to connect with by salting your home stream with tweets from users you are not connected with. You also show up in home feeds of people you are yet to connect with. It is, after all, a social medium.

A second way that people might come to view your profile is by clicking the "Who to Follow" option and seeing suggestions similar to those they are already following. Twitter provides this very useful option to help users find people similar to those they are already following.

A third way that someone might get to view your profile is as a result of a search that they initiated. Let's say that a user is interested in 'dog trainers' for some reason. They enter the term into the search box and, low and behold, Twitter provides them with a list of all profiles that contain the words 'dog trainer'.

A fourth way that your profile might get viewed is if another user recommends that you connect with one of their contacts.

No matter how, let's assume that a user has found their way to your profile. The first thing that they see is your summary profile. It's the one that pops up when they click on your user name and it shows your Twitter presence – your front door, as it were. They see a brief overview. On the top half of the display they see your avatar, header photo, bio and a tally of tweets, followers and users you follow. Below that, there's a 'followed by' field that appears if anyone the user follows also follows you. Below all that, there is a summary which displays your two latest tweets.

Now, let's say that our inquisitive user is intrigued by your profile summary but the finger is still hesitating above the 'follow' button. They have the option of clicking the 'go to full profile' to find out more before making a decision to follow or not. Although it's safe to assume that most will make up their minds from your Profile Summary screen, in my experience, those who visit your full profile are more likely to be 'keepers' – followers of value.

All of this means that you need to make the most of the screen space available to you, maximize the impact of your images, make sure your bio reads well and ensure that your Tweets attract the kind of followers you want.

Let the Tweeting Begin

Now that you've got your profile up, you are looking at your home feed page and there is this empty box in the upper left. It has a capacity of 140 characters and right now it is blank. This is when you start establishing your Twitter brand; building on your profile. It's also the moment when you can begin adding to the conversation. The importance of your decisions at this point cannot be overstated when it comes to defining how you will fare in the ebb and flow of social media.

As will all social media, Twitter is mostly about branding – establishing yours or your company's in such a way that that the return on the effort involved is strongly positive. Few people look at it this way and it leads to all sorts of wasted time and money. Like everything else you do, there is outgo and income – costs and benefits. Maybe both are intangibles; like when you volunteer for charity work but, if Twitter is going to be worth the effort, it has to pay off in some way.

The minute that you start filling that empty box with

characters, you open a conversation with people who are seeing your Tweets in their home feed. Their first impression of you is reading something that you have taken the time to write and send out into the Twitterverse. From that first encounter, they begin to build an image of you. Think about it as a first impression that grows with further encounters – that is, if further encounters are welcome.

This last point is one that most users of Twitter spend pitifully little time thinking about. Because Twitter is so easy to start using, a lot of people give little thought to how they use it and what, if any, benefits they are receiving from participation. As a result they do far more harm to their personal or corporate branding than they realize. In this chapter, I want to highlight some of the ways that damage is done in the hope that, with that knowledge, you can avoid shooting yourself in the foot while training for a marathon. For those of you who don't know what a meadow muffin is, I'll leave the discovery of meaning to you. A simple search will give you all you need to know. Here are just a few that you need to avoid.

Twenty-One Meadow Muffins to Step In

1. Don't Think About It

Most experienced Twitter users look for people to connect with who have a focus that interests them. Users without any apparent focus are generally seen as a waste of time. The 'all things to all people' accounts are mostly ignored. If you don't work to coordinate your profile and your Tweets with your list of followers – to build a following that resonates with your stated purpose for being on Twitter – people will see you as so much cannon fodder – Twitter noise. As an example, I regularly view the followers and followed list of people I am thinking about connecting to. The best experience is when I see four or five people per page that I would also like to connect with. This is a high-quality connection for me. The other end of the spectrum is the user with lists full of hookers, halfwits and scammers. In those situations, I reach for the handle and flush the commode. Most often I 'Block' them for good measure.

2. Talk But Don't Listen

What part of 'Social Media' don't you understand? Is Twitter a place where you mouth off and ignore what other people say? Do you routinely post Tweets and never, or seldom, read what others have posted. Is Twitter just an opportunity to parade your ego in public? In social media, people who are self-obsessed are generally seen as wallpaper. It is a sad thing to see any person moving through life without engaging with their fellow travelers. You need to realize that the very people you are blasting with your Tweets are judging you as a potential connection. They will be more likely to see you in a positive light if you regularly engage others in conversations.

3. Be Negative

This behavior is often taken as evidence of repressed adolescence. I see profiles that say, "If you don't follow me back, I will unfollow." Other profiles contain foul or abusive language. Recently I saw a number of profiles that stated, "The opinions are mine." That was the entire profile. Well, that really told me a lot about the user; didn't it? Needless to say, I went looking elsewhere. If you come off as angry or irritated, most people will ignore you. You don't have to be Mary Poppins. Just be yourself and, if you are a reflexively negative person, perhaps social media is not for you.

4. Get Hacked

You want to look like a complete schmuck? You want to show people that you are careless and a pain in the butt at the same time. Well, here's you big chance. Have your Twitter account hacked and an have army of amoral morons flood the home feeds of your 'friends' with all sorts of vile messages. If you can't protect your own account with basic security measures, what kind of a connection would you be?

5. Oversell: You're an 'innovative, cutting edge, highly creative, internationally known, widely recognized, thought leading, highly sought after expert in your field.'

The only people who use any of these words to describe themselves almost certainly aren't deserving of them. As an old friend used to say, "People who routinely break their arm patting themselves on the back were crippled in the cradle." Do you really want a potential follower's first impression to be "Well, this guy sure is alleged in his own mind?"

6. Write a profile with no content

You can see evidence of this particular meadow muffin as your home feed grows. You will encounter users who don't bother to tell you anything about themselves. What does that tell you about them? Others seem to think that a pale attempt at wit is called for. Remember, this is social media. The key word, as I have said before, is social. For the most part, Twitter is about people relating to other people. If you put forth an avatar without content, be prepared to be treated as irrelevant and immaterial. The extreme of this one is the profile that is completely blank. Yes, there are Twitter users with completely blank profiles. Many of them are robo-accounts.

7. Write your bio in third person.

"We are not amused." You've no doubt heard that one before. Who are you, the Queen? I am always amazed when I encounter users whose profile seems to be written by someone about someone else. Writing in the third person makes you look pompous and imperious. It's like you couldn't be bothered yourself so you asked someone else to write it. Even if you're Twitter account was established for professional reasons, remember Twitter is a personal, social platform and your profile should reflect that. Your profile should induce the kinds of people you want to connect with to connect with you.

8. Be an egg or worse a cartoon character

This one really drives me nuts. The egg look is the default on Twitter. It is what you get when you first set up your account. Using it makes you look either like a bot – a computer generated account used to fool people into thinking that they are connected with a real person – or someone who just doesn't get it or doesn't care. But you can do worse than the egg. Choose a cartoon character for an avatar. Yeah, that will make you seem worth connecting with. Look, you want to be a Klingon, that's fine if you want to connect with Trekkies whose life is also a cartoon. But, if you want something more out of Twitter, try being yourself. You only have a few chances to engage people visually on Twitter and only one chance to make a first impression, so don't waste it. The best alternative is either a genuine picture of you or your company logo.

9. **Emphasize things in your profile are of no interest to desired followers**

If you are looking to build a following based on your religious preferences, for example, by all means start your profile with a statement of that preference. But you need to realize that lots of potential followers not particularly interested in religion will read your profile and decide to look elsewhere. If you define yourself by your religion you will most likely be avoided by people who don't share your beliefs. Most Twitter users will avoid proselytizers of a theology. If you start your profile contending that you are a family man, realize that such an introduction will probably filter your connections in that direction. Remember, you have only a brief time to advance a summary of yourself and your interests. Make sure that you choose the words that will attract the interest of those you want to connect with.

10. Your Tweets have no interesting content about you and your interests

There are users who send out a shower of Tweets containing quotes from famous people. I suppose that they see themselves as providing inspiration to followers. But most potential followers will come to the conclusion that you have nothing to say or add to a conversation. "People who have nothing to say frequently fall into quoting others." One particularly irritating application will publish 'your journal' and broadcast to your followers that the 'latest issue is out'. The first time I saw one of these Tweet, I clicked on the link - since it mentioned that I was featured in the journal. It was pure crap. The user had nothing to do with the journal other than to lend their name. The journal was publishing articles and collecting on the click-thru traffic. And my home feed was being cluttered by this junk. Well, it isn't being cluttered any more. I routinely disconnect from people who hypocritically publish 'their journal'. Other users seem to think that followers are fascinated by information about what they had for breakfast or what their kids did at school. It's possible to build a following of people like that. Just make sure that is what you want in return for your efforts.

11. Post the same Tweets over and over and over again

Users who have discovered applications that repeatedly Tweet the same messages are easy to spot. You see the same text over and over from them. In social media terms, this means that they prefer automated Tweets to actual engagement with followers. Think of the message you are sending when you do this. How likely is it that someone is going to respond to you as a person when what they see is machine generated? Twitter is all about people engaging with other people. Automated responses will fall on deaf ears and your Tweets will go unnoticed and responded to.

12. Be an anti-humanist opportunist

Remember that people are getting to know you through your Tweets. They've never met you and are unlikely to ever do so. If you are clearly on some sort of ideological crusade or maniacally spreading some gospel according to you or someone else, most users will quickly realize that they really don't matter to you as anything other than a potential convert. The worst of these offenders are political hacks that routinely barf the latest party line. Your network of followers will quickly accumulate the likeminded and those who you might value connecting with will avoid being preached to.

13. Use one of those irritating 'validation' apps

This is one of my pet peeves. I refer to these people as true twitter twits. If I want to connect with them, I am required to prove that I am a human being. (By the way, I have no way of knowing if they are what I am being asked to prove.) Some of the applications are truly irritating. I am asked to respond to a situation that requires me to respond by filling in a text box. But many of those situations force me to view advertisements and respond by expressing adulation for the company that has purchased the ad. Unless there is a good reason for me to want to connect with a particular person, I avoid such connections. By using such an application, you make it that much more difficult to connect with you. Beyond that, you may appear to be paranoid about something that potential connections know is not a major problem. Asking a person to jump through a hoop before you will connect with them can give that impression and it is a poor way to start off a relationship.

14. Follow, and/or be followed by, hookers, halfwits and scammers

Many new Twitter users never think that someone who is deciding to invite a connection will go to their list of followers and see who they have accepted. But the more advanced users do just that. I have found some users whose follower list is made up almost completely of hookers, halfwits and scammers. Needless to say, I was not very interested in connecting with them. Other users have lists of followers that include Tweets in languages that the user clearly doesn't speak. Viewing a user's follower list is one of the best ways to get a clearer idea about who they are and what they intend. The same is true of the list of people they follow. Think of it this way, someone visits your profile page and clicks on the list of your followers. Their first impression is that it is a trash pile of hookers, halfwits and scammers. Now likely do you think they would be to see you are someone they want to connect with?

15. Be all about the numbers

This approach is a close relative to the last one. Some users think that Twitter is all about building a big following no matter what its composition. As a result they follow anybody and accept any followers. Think about how this might make someone who is considering you as a connection feel. If they see you as collecting scalps, they may not want to volunteer to make your ego swell a bit more. Also, remember that the Tweets of anyone you follow will show up in your home feed and can show up on the home feeds of those who are following you. A regular stream of Tweets offering racy photos in exchange for an email address will turn off the more serious of your followers and brand you as a promulgator of pornography. One of most potent options that Twitter gives you is the 'Block' button. If you click on the down arrow next to any user, one of the options that you find is to block them. I use this button regularly to screen out hookers, halfwits, scammers and scalp hunters.

16. Market followers or some other scam

If you are all about the numbers, these people will be like drug dealers for you. They offer to add to your follower list in exchange for a payment. Most of them are identify thieves trolling for people who are dumb enough to provide personal and payment information. The accounts that they add are almost certainly machine generated. In the end, you risk having your identity stolen and turn your followers list into a sewer. Remember, Twitter isn't about following blindly. It's about building your own stream of content that's interesting and ultimately tailored to you. If you're following everyone just because they follow you, you're diluting your Twitter stream with content that may not be of interest, and ultimately cheapening the value of your own brand. Remember that potential followers might visit your followers list. What message about you does it send if what they see in a lot of users flogging offers to increase followings?

17. Your following ratio is out of whack

It is hard for a new Twitter user to get used to the fact that the tracks they leave I the social media landscape can be viewed by potential followers. A lopsided ratio of users you follow to users who follow you is often a red flag that you are either spamming or that your Tweets are duller than white bread. It's understandable — and expected — that you will be following more accounts than are following you. It's the ratio that is important. A large disparity in these numbers makes your profile look suspicious. You should be gathering followers methodically and building a following that reflects and serves your interests. Don't go crazy with the "Follow" button.

18. Tweet too much or all at once

There are users who just can't seem to take a break from tweeting. I have seen some who flood my home feed with ten to twenty Tweets at such a pace that they are all one after another. This is called spamming. Stepping in the spammer meadow muffin is a sure way for you to get in the Twitter dog house.

19. Tweet and Retweet Yourself

If you pay attention to your home feed you may see a pattern that, at first, you may not believe. The first thing you may notice is that there are people who retweet their retweeted tweets. Apparently they are so amazed that somebody might find something they tweeted interesting that they just have to tell the world. If you look closer, you may see that there are people who respond to their own tweets. In effect, they are talking to themselves by themselves. It's a good idea not to appear this shallow. The very people who you are hoping to connect with are probably the ones who will notice that you just can't seem to get enough of yourself.

20. Robots craft your tweets.

There are applications available that will schedule your tweets. If you use WordPress, for example, there are lots of plugins that will allow you to send out Tweets automatically. Unlike some authors, I am not necessarily against using them. The issue is not the scheduling but the content. Remember, in social media, content is king and relevant content is the platinum standard. If your recent tweets look like they were automatically generated, people will be less likely to follow you.

Some applications allow you to send out a greeting to people who decided to follow you. For the most part, these greetings are round-filed without being read. People will connect with you – allow you into their home feed – because they expect to see interesting Tweets from you. They want to hear your genuine voice, in real time. They don't want lofty quotes that you've scheduled to go live at strategic periods, stats from your latest workout or what your top stories are via a third-party application. Remember, Twitter is about engagement, not just broadcasting meaningless words. If you don't reply to other Twitter users, or otherwise react to tweets and trending topics you see in your stream, you're wasting your time and theirs.

21. Be constantly selling something.

If every Tweet by a particular user is a sales pitch, people will tune out quickly. The best Tweets intrigue your followers and stimulate them to respond. The best result from any of your Tweets is that it starts a conversation. A direct sales pitch is a great way to shut down that possibility right out of the box. If you're using Twitter to sell something in a crude manner, people will not follow you. There is sufficient unwelcome advertising out there already.

Well, those should get you thinking about how to avoid self-sabotage. Now let's turn to some techniques that you can use to avoid some of those pesky meadow muffins.

Gut Checking Your Twitter Presence

Are You a Social Networking Slob?

OK, now you have a Twitter account. You are tweeting away. Your followers list is building nicely and you are following a fairly coherent group of users. It's time to take a look at the tracks you have been leaving in the snow. I want to focus on social media and its usefulness in developing a virtual presence and expanding your branding footprint. Let's take a closer look at your Twitter account. Superficially it may appear that things are fine. You have an expanded presence. But when we start to drill down the proverbial wheels may start to fall off.

Isn't that Tweet?

By now you may have several hundred, or even several thousand, followers. Call up your list of followers. Several patterns may become immediately noticeable:

- **Advertising for Scammers**: Does your list contained a large number of what can only be termed 'are you stupid enough to fall for this crap' followers. Most of these scammers offer to increase your following for a payment of money. True, there are always people moronic enough to trade their personal data for a raft of meaningless, temporary followers but this was not the point. I would put it this way, "Every one of the Tweets that these people post show up in your feed and all of your followers see them. By forwarding them, you are saying 'this is something that you, my followers, ought to see'. You have set yourself up as an advertising agency for scammers. What does that say to your followers about you?" This is question that may never have occurred to you. People who followed you see your time-line feed and will probably come to some judgments about you based on that experience.

- **What Language is That**? The second pattern is the presence of lots of followers who were posting in a language that you clearly do not speak. Now, I welcome the diversity of Twitter and the inclusion of many cultures but what's the point of having and forwarding followers you can't understand? What does that say about your definition of 'followers'? Is your feed full of all sorts of strange looking characters making words that you can't translate?

- **Hookers and Halfwits**: A third pattern might be found in your feed. Remember, your feed is a reflection of who you associate with and the kind of Tweets you approve of. After all, it's your feed! What does it say about you if that feed is full of women with their breasts hanging out, cursing adolescents and people ranting about their own particular crusade? You are, after all, promoting their tweets by including them in your feed.

- **Paranoia on Parade**: The forth pattern might be your use of a 'validation' service to identify 'validated accounts'. Most people who use these obscenities have little experience in responding to their requests. One in particular 'filter' has sold ads which they use as validation questions. So you get to praise the advantages of this service or that product before your account can be 'validated'. Two points here. First, given the amount of crap accounts on Twitter, how effective do you think this kind of bush league screening is? And second, what does it say about you and your attitude towards people who might want to follow you? "Nice doggie, jump through this demeaning hoop!"

OK, I'll stop at four. I figure you get the picture. If you don't, five won't help. If you see these patterns in your Twitter feed, major changes should occur. If you find that one out of four or five tweets in your feed were from scammers selling followers, many are in a language you don't speak or read (Surely it occurs to you that you have no way of telling what these people were saying), what is that saying about you? If there is also a heavy smattering of hookers and halfwits, what is that doing to your brand? It's time of a great purge. You may end up blocking hundred accounts outright and un-following hundreds more. In the end, your list of followers will start to make sense and communicate to people who you are and what you are interested in. Your new follows will start to make sense. The days of building an ever-higher trash pile are over.

It's Social Networking Stupid!

But there may be a far more serious problem with your approach to social networking. You may not be social at all when it comes to Tweeting. Twitter provides an opportunity to comment whenever the mood moves you to. The essence of social networking is regular exchanges between members. You may be completely absent when it came to being social.

I am fond of observing that the journey towards wisdom begins with the discovery of at least one non-instrumental reason why there are other people on the planet. Not every interaction has to connect directly to some purpose. People chat. They banter. Sometimes they inform. At other times they are informed. The percentage of participants in social networks that understand this simple truth is depressingly low. Otherwise, how could the 'we'll sell you 5,000 followers for $50' scammers make a living? How could the 'we'll increase your friends for only $40' crowd prosper? They do you know. They do because there are thousands of anti-social types swimming against the current and ripe for the scamming.

Cleaning up your Twitter feed should be a real eye-opening journey. When you come to the conclusion that your participation in social networks may be negatively branding you and limiting the benefits you receive from the time you spent on them, it's time for a change. When you realize that people who are thinking of connecting with you may start by looking at who you are connected to and what they were posting, you may come to an important realization. You can change all that. Things can change – and for the best.

Now it's your turn. Take a look at your Twitter feed. What does it say about you? Are you a promoter of scammers? Are you pimping for hookers and halfwits? Are you blindly passing on tweets in languages you can't even recognize let alone understand?

Are your 'friends' just convenient name tags for people you don't know and couldn't care less about? Do you think any of them give a momentary thought to who you are? Do you give a damn about who they are? Believe me when I tell you that people who see your feed and lists will come to that conclusion on their own.

Take a good look at your entire Twitter presence. What does your social media footprint say about you as a person? Are you an engaged participant or a parasite? Are you a facilitator of the least – a pimp for the ethically challenged – or an honest and sincere presence? Are you a social networking slob?

Twitter the Right Way

When considering what to post about today go to your home feed and see what your 'friends' are posting. You may get a few good ideas. One may stand out. Maybe it is echoed by more than one person. Say you find a Tweet like this:

With the increase in business use on Twitter, how do you stand out from the crowd without looking like "Buy my product, give me money" etc.? It seems like it's getting super crowded these days.

Maybe another user chimes in:

I agree. I purposely don't have a twitter account linked to my business. I don't know how to stand out without being obnoxious about it.

You have stumbled onto a conversation. These are the most important types of threads in Twitter. After reading these comments, you might think back to how you use Twitter and how you have changed with experience. You want to have great conversations with friends, and even built strong business relationships. Maybe you've spent more time on other platforms and Twitter has taken a back seat. Perhaps you use it mostly to share content, yours and others, and don't converse with others the way you should. That should bother you. Maybe you have noticed a lot of your business friends have been pulling away and falling into the same trap. This thread brings another option to mind. Your feed is too cluttered with noise – Tweets that don't advance your branding. Has what began as much more of a personal platform to establish and extend your brand has been taken over by people who just want to shout and sell? Perhaps you're part of the problem

Is there a better way?

Let's say you're a small business owner and you want to use Twitter to advance the brand of that company. How can you use it effectively? Here are a few suggestions for how you can actually be effective on Twitter without contributing to the noise:

1. Have a proper understanding of the platform

Twitter, like most social media, is not about immediate results. It's more about planning and the long term; about building relationships. This doesn't happen overnight. It's incredibly important to have the right mindset and expectations. If you expect a rapid ROI, you'll get frustrated and it won't work for you.

2. Cultivate a following

I chose the word "cultivate" very carefully. Understand who your customers are, and find them. Begin by finding your existing customers. Then move on to those who are in your physical geographic location, and also in your chosen field. Follow them in hopes that they will follow back. In other words, choose those you follow carefully. Don't just look to beef up your numbers. Relevant followers are more important than big numbers. Also be sure to follow anyone who starts a conversation with you or Retweets your tweets. If they are taking the time to do that, they have at least some level of interest in what you have to say.

3. Twitter doesn't exist in a vacuum

I say this about all social platforms and social media in general. Integrate everything. If you're going to be on Twitter, find ways to let your customers know about it, even if it's offline. Tell them on your website. Tell them about your printed material. Tell them on Facebook and your other social properties. Don't treat Twitter, or any social media platform, for that matter, as a stand-alone.

4. Share great content

If you want people to be interested in what you have to say, start by sharing great content. Some of that will hopefully be your own content in the form of Tweets, but also be generous in sharing and retweeting other content that you like. By sharing great content, you'll build your reputation as someone not only to be followed, but someone whose links should be clicked on. By doing so, you are not only a content creator, but a content curator. People will find you useful.

5. Don't be one-dimensional

This is something else I harp on. One of my friends is an artist. For her, it's natural to not only tweet about her work, but the work of fellow artists, as well as articles about art. But she doesn't stop there. She might tweet about music, or food, or any other topic that interests her. Just because you have an area of expertise doesn't mean that's all you think about. We all have a variety of interests, and so do your followers. Not everything you tweet will interest all of them, but by being well rounded, they will see you as human, and not just someone who is shouting all the time about what they are selling.

6. Converse

Again, common sense, and it ties into that buzzword: engage. But seriously, this is at the heart of social media: being social. Talk to people. Start conversations. Respond to them. Yeah, it's become trite to use the word "engage," but it's true. That's how we build relationships and get to know people. You will make so many great friends over Twitter, some of whom will become clients. It won't happen overnight, but it will happen. They will get to know you, and eventually some of them want to work with you. And not all of those conversations should be about what you do. Remember point 5. You might tweet about food, sports, your family, your town, and a lot of other things.

Remember, it is a conversation, a dialogue, not a monologue. You're not just there to yell into the ether. Contribute to the conversation and engage in dialogue.

7. Be present

To really get into Twitter and do it well, you need to be there. You need to make a commitment. This isn't something you put on a check list and schedule a block of time for. You need to be there; often and regularly. You can be on Twitter most of the days without really making it a time drain. With mobile technology and the right apps you can be there and converse without too much interruption into your day. Over time it will become a normal part of your everyday routine, just like the conversations you have with those around you.

8. Personal before business

I don't have any hard and fast evidence for this, just my observations: the people who use Twitter best are the ones who are there as themselves before they are there representing their business. Be yourself. You are much better at Twitter when you're representing yourself. It's not that you're not representing my business, but your mindset is different. When you are there as you, you are less interested in "selling" and pushing your message out there. So just be yourself. Converse in the same way you would converse in person or in public. Don't over think it.

9. Don't think about marketing

This goes along with the last one, but the reason so many individuals and businesses end up shouting and getting too salesy on Twitter is that they think of it as a marketing tool. It's not. It is a communications tool. Sure, it can be used for marketing, but it's really for all types of communication. Build relationships and provide customer service. Ask questions and do research. Answer questions for others. If all you do is focus on marketing, you'll get boring really fast. Like I said earlier, most of this is common sense. And in some ways this is both the simplest and the hardest thing to do. Don't spend so much time worrying about how effective you're being, and focus on just being you, and communicating well with others.

The Most Valuable Tips You'll Ever Get about Using Social Media

Most people who use any of the social media sites do it poorly and without any serious thought. I spend a lot of time coaching others on how to make the most of the potential of social media. During those engagements, I have seen a number of recurring patterns that, if avoided, greatly increase the benefits you get from time spent.

One of the reasons that people experience poor results from social media sites is that it is so easy to get started and even easier to get sucked up in what seems like the its principal advantage – the ability to make lots of new connections. This seduction is the same no matter which of the many very good sites you are using. What is true for Twitter is also true for Facebook and Linked In.

Reflexive Response

I'd like to focus on Twitter; although, as I've said, the experience for most users is the same across the social media platforms. If you have a Twitter account, think about what it was like when you first set it up. You had no followers and, even when you began to get some, the numbers grew depressingly slowly.

Now Twitter, like all the other sites, realizes that a large number of relatively unconnected accounts does not make for a very vital social network. They help you to expand your network by suggesting others that you might want to connect with. This is a great service as it looks at the connections that you have and suggests similar ones.

Of course, there is a downside that you will almost immediately discover. If you initial contact list is full of hookers, halfwits and scammers, that's what you will get as suggestions. However, if you spend some effort building a focused group of followers, Twitter will help you get more like the ones you have. Your reflexive response is to build your numbers as quickly as possible. Most people are relatively unselective at first as they try to make it to the first major level – having at least two thousand followers. But remember the old acronym – GIGO – garbage in, garbage out!

Being Selective Yields Coherence

It makes no difference if you have a few hundred followers or several thousand. The issue is how relevant each follower is to your interests. One of the best ways to maximize your return from your social media accounts is to develop a carefully thought out set of criteria for the contacts; then use those criteria to select new contacts. It also makes great sense to spend some time on a regular schedule pruning the tree – unfollowing those on your lists that don't meet those criteria.

Here's a way to think of the process. You are building a very valuable list of contacts, friends and followers. The better job you do the more valuable the list will be. Be selective and the return from your efforts will increase.

Avoid Negatively Branding Yourself

Here's one of those suggestions that can improve your experience. If you are indiscriminate in selecting your followers, your list will reflect that tendency and people who take the time to check you list will think far less of you as a potential contact. The fact is that, much like your business card, your social media presence brands you. Potential contacts gauge you by the kind of people you are connected with. What do you think they will think of you if your list is full of hookers, halfwits and scammers? What does it say about you if there are lots of very negative people among your followers? What does it say about you if your Tweets are full of vitriol and sarcasm? Negativity will negatively brand you.

It Isn't the Quantity it's the Quality

Remember, its 'social' media and 'social' networking. A very high percentage of users on any of the social media platforms just do not seem to realize that. Your presence is defined by your contributions. By far the best and fastest way to build your contact list is to provide a regular flow of postings that are interesting to the kinds of people you want to connect with. A few high-quality tweets will go long way to advancing your brand and presenting yourself as someone who others want to associate with.

As logical as you might find that statement, you need to look hard into a mirror. You need to look at your contributions. Take a close look at your Tweets. If you were the kind of person you want to connect with, would you find them interesting enough to follow the person who is posting them? Remember that your Tweets occasionally show up in the time lines of people you are not presently connected with. That's another way that organizations like Twitter facilitate the development of vital social networks. Look at your Tweets. Would you follow you?

Your Interest in What Other People Post is as Important as What You Post

One of the great sins that most people commit on social media sites is to see only one lane on a two way street. They constantly blare out their Tweets, for instance, and spend no time at all reading the ones that their followers post. Now maybe that makes sense to you but it seems stump dumb to me. Why would you put in effort to build a network of followers only to ignore what they have to say? Are you so self-absorbed that such a question is a non-sequitur? Doesn't such an attitude seem a tad self-centered to you?

The truth is that the vast majority of users of social media are exactly that – self-centered non-sequiturs. They don't matter because they have a purely instrumental attitude towards other people in their network. If you are not prepared to be social, how can you expect to get much out of social media?

Make the Change and Reap the Rewards

I try to update my status or make a contribution on all of the social media networks I use daily. I highly recommend the practice. I also spend time reading the postings of people that have caught my interest. Very often I respond to them; either with a compliment or an added comment. And I try to bring interesting articles, news events and poll to the attention of my contacts. You will be surprised at the results if you adopt these approaches.

Twitter, Skype and Facebook Vulnerabilities

Now let's focus on a particular vulnerability of Twitter and some other social networks.

Twitter Baited

Twitter allows you to be notified when you get new followers. For those of you who have the option set, your inbox becomes a more interesting place. Twitter tells you when you have new followers and whether you are following them. The notification comes in the form of an email sent to your primary account. I have found this service to be very useful. It gives me the basic information on new followers and, if I am not currently following them, a link to log on and elect to do so. It also makes it easy to decide not to follow a particular account. If that's the case, I just do nothing. After going down the list of new followers, I delete the message. It's clean and fast.

Lately I have been noticing that the service, while incredibly useful, seems to have a blind spot. If you read the prior chapters you will recognize the term 'scammer' as I used it. The term refers to people who 'sell' followers. They will promise you thousands of new followers for some amount of money. I take it as evidence that there are fools dumb enough to fall for these traps that the scams appear to be spreading.

If you want to see what I mean, just peruse the Twitter accounts of some of your followers. Many of them suffer from a rash of hucksters running this kind of scam. A recent account that I reviewed had every fifth follower running a version of this scam. Needless to say, I un-followed that user.

These scammers run their scams because they are profitable. They run them partially because inconsiderate slobs like the user I just mentioned give the scammers lots of free publicity. After all, this person accepted the scammers as followers. They must be legitimate. (Of course, I opt for the obverse conclusion. "This user accepted the scammers as followers. I don't want to, in any way, be connected with people like him.")

The second reason that these scammers flourish is that their operation has almost no costs associated with it and there are a percentage of people using Twitter who are simply too stupid to avoid the scam. So, criminals flourish. The question is, are you helping them. Another question is, "Is Twitter working to shut them down or facilitate their activities". And that beings me to the blind spot.

Recently I have been getting a lot of followers who write in Cyrillic scrip. They seem to come in waves, mostly late at night and those waves have increased lately. They were all new accounts with no, or almost no, followers. I routinely blocked them and that, as they say, is that. But I have noticed something strange that has caused me to change my approach. None of these followers have ever shown up on notices that I receive from Twitter. Saying it another way, Twitter seems to be unaware of new followers of a certain type.

I've looked at a few of these accounts to see what they had in common. They seem to be clone accounts with few followers and repetitive tweets. I suspect that they are the results of 'scammers account cloning mills'. "You want thousands of followers? OK, send me $50 and I will get them for you. Oh Alexei, run off a couple thousand accounts. I've got a moron who just sent us $50."

My question is, "Why aren't these new followers showing up on the Twitter emails?" I don't pretend to have an answer to that question but one possibility is that the scammers have figured a way around having them listed. Certainly, if Twitter knew that this kind of thing was happening, they would shut it down. It does, after all, significantly degrade user experience. We won't know until Twitter becomes aware of this situation. So, here's my suggestion. Instead of just blocking the scammers and the bogus accounts, block and report as spam. It is the option directly below 'block'. That's the change I have made.

There is another kind of vulnerability that you can find working in both Facebook and Skype. I call it the 'furtive greeting'. You get a message from someone you don't know. Most often it contains something short like 'Hi' or 'Dearest'. Sometimes the message is longer and, occasionally, it is an outright 'advance fee' scam. These are people using the equivalent of slave labor to send out thousands of these kinds of messages from thousands of different accounts. They are trolling for idiots.

Unlike Twitter, neither Facebook nor Skype provides a way to shut down the rain of trollers. I actually got to a human being at Skype (yes, I know, I should feel honored that the company actually recognized me as a human being and deigned to have another human actually talk to me). I was told that there was no way for me to block these incoming requests. They were, in a real sense, defending the right of the scammer to tempt me. Facebook offers the same type of enabling. I daily receive virtually the same messages through my Facebook account.

Until these companies give us the ability to screen out unwanted messages, the only recourse is to bounce, block and report them.

Personal Responsibility and Social Media

So, that's my rant for today. I hope you've found it useful. I would leave you with one thing to think about. Your active or passive approach to these kinds of situations helps define how the various social media platforms evolve. If you just passively take whatever comes down the pike, you are contributing to the rise of scammers, hookers and halfwits. Your tombstone will read "Here lays a real enabler." If, on the contrary, you actively participate in efforts to improve social media it will read, "Here lies someone who set out to make a difference and did!" Your choice. Slime or climb?

Cleaning Up Your Twitter Account

In an earlier chapter (Are You a Social Networking Slob), I described how being a slob when it comes to social networking can damage your personal brand. I had published a similar article some time ago. The response to the article was very strong. I got lots of emails from people who never stopped to think about the damage they were doing to their own brand. One email summed up the common theme. "*I always thought that social networking was a game of numbers. I never stopped to think about the quality of my network; only the quantity. Your article opened my eyes and I didn't like what I saw. So how do I clean this mess up?*"

Here are a few tips to help you clean up your list of followers and make Twitter a positive, rather than negative, contributor to your personal brand.

Revisit Your Profile: Let's start with your profile. Although it's true that most Twitter users don't spend much time looking at profiles (to them you are just another brick in the wall), the ones that do may be important as followers. So, is your photo one of you in a goofy hat or of some cartoon character? What impression does the text of your profile convey? Do you come off as a serious and focused individual (remember, even comedians can be serious about their art)? Take the time to think about what you want to accomplish by having a Twitter account and then produce a profile that advances that interest. Above all, your profile should be an authentic reflection of who you are.

Cruise Your Timeline: Now it's time to begin scraping off the scammers, hookers, halfwits and the unintelligible. Set aside a few minutes every day for a week or so. (After a week things will be cleared up substantially) Pick out the bad apples and unfollow them. Block the truly rotten ones. At first you will probably be shocked at the number of users that you want to rid yourself of. Remember, scammers, hookers, halfwits and the unintelligible are generally in the business of polluting your timeline as often as possible. Their profits depend on your assistance. This is particularly true of scammers who are 'selling' followers. Your willingness to help them get the word out is something that they depend on. It makes no difference to them whether your support is active or a result of indifference or inattention as long as they can show up in your home feed and those of all your followers. Go at it with a vengeance. Initially you will scrape a lot of dog dirt off your shoes. Keep at it and the skies will clear.

Choose Who You Follow Carefully: There is no sense of adding to a mess you are working to clean one up. Followers will show up and you will face four options. One, you could follow them back. Two, you could not follow them back and take no other action. Three, you could block them. Four, you could block them and report them as a spammer. You will have to form your own strategy but here is what I do:

1.   I look at the profile of the person who has followed me and ask the simple question "Is this the kind of person that I want to be associated with?" I almost always check their list of followers and those they are following. If I find lots of people on those lists that attract my interest, that is a major plus. I ask myself, is this person presenting a brand that is serious and focused. If the answers are yes, I follow them back.

2.   If the answer is no, I then consider why I don't want to be associated with. If it is merely not a good fit with my interests, I simply don't follow them back.

That means that their tweets will not show up in my timeline but mine will in theirs – at least until they unfollow me.

3.   If I decide that the new follower falls into one of the scammers, hookers, halfwits and the unintelligible categories but is not insidious in intent, I block them. I do this a lot with the unintelligible. BTW, be prepared for a bit of blowback. When I started blocking a particular language, I got a sharp increase in followers posting in that language. It seems I'd struck a nerve. You see, the scammers meet their 'quota of new followers' by creating thousands of new 'straw man' accounts. A group of these scammers was apparently creating massive numbers of accounts in this particular language. I was messing with their scam. For a while I blocked lots of 'new followers'. But, eventually, the scammers figured out that I wasn't buying onto their scam and went away.

4.   Finally, if I decide that the new follower has some sort of hidden, insidious agenda, I block and report them as a spammer I routinely do this with the 'we'll get you thousands of new followers for $Xs' crowd. I figure that I'm helping to clean up the community and twitter in the process. If Twitter receives enough of these reports, they may take the step of shutting them down.

Choose Who You Follow Carefully – Part Two: Twitter has a wonderful service that will help you better select people and organizations to follow. They will suggest them based on similarities with the users that you already follow. Of course, if your list of followers is a steaming pile of cow flop, their suggestions will further soil the nest. But, once you get your list cleaned up, Twitter can help you further refine your list. They want to help you connect with a high-quality network of followers. The more refined your list, the better their suggestions.

Here is a suggestion that might help. Go to your timeline and scan down until you find a tweet that is particularly useful. Then take a look at the profile of the tweeter. When the profile pops up, you will see the most recent tweets, number of followers and how many they are following. (Avoid people who are followed but not following. These people are almost always alleged in their own mind and not interests in anyone but themselves.) If this looks like an interesting person, click on their followers. This will take you to a list of people who you might like to follow and who might reciprocate. You can then move down the list and 'Follow' people and organizations that match your interests. The better you do in selecting accounts to follow, the more focused your list of followers will become and the more relevant your average follower will be to your interests.

Understand Your Objectives: In the end, the most positive thing that you can do is develop a clear understanding of why you are using social networking. Most people skip over this most important step and wade right in. You should have a written 'statement of purpose' that will serve as your guide. Remember the words of Yogi Berra, "*If you don't know where you're going, how will you know when you get there?*" Social networking should not be a mindless reflex but a focused and purposeful undertaking.

Twitter Etiquette

Making Your Content Special is the Best Etiquette

Twitter is a great way to introduce potential customers to your product brand, and both large and small businesses have taken to the social media network in order to promote their company, sell more products, and increase their brand's reputation and profile. The number of businesses now reaching out through Twitter has increased massively in the last few years, and there have been notable successes.

However, there have also been some setbacks, with small companies and marketers finding that they struggle to sell their brand name on Twitter, and have few followers who are interested in the company as a business. The biggest problem that small businesses have is that they are so keen to push their products that they fail to observe even the most basic of Twitter etiquette rules. This drives people away, and also negatively impacts the company's reputation. There are several things which a business can do to improve their reputation on Twitter. Perhaps the most important element of this is to carefully examine their content, and make sure that it meets the rules of Twitter Etiquette for businesses.

How Twitter Etiquette Can Make or Damage Reputations

Twitter is an enormous social network that links people across the globe. Businesses often choose to join Twitter based on this large customer potential, but they fail to realize that they are essentially marketing themselves in public. They ignore Twitter etiquette because they view their account as being in a private world, where they are not likely to offend or cause controversy. In fact, Twitter is less like an isolated bubble of private comment, and more like a public stage, where thousands of people can see what the business is saying at any point. Therefore, the first rule of Twitter etiquette has to be remembering that you are speaking to people who may not know or understand you, and who are unlikely to appreciate your sense of humor. Businesses should remember the rule to Twitter etiquette that they should not Tweet anything that they would want to keep private, or that they would not want strangers to read.

Twitter etiquette also requires that your posts be polite and able to withstand being part of a permanent record. Businesses can't remove those Tweets from public view, and so they need to be aware that everything they say can be viewed by thousands of people not only in the present, but also in the future, too. A public fight on Twitter can quickly travel around the world, with screen grabs recording your comments for posterity. It is essential to remember the rule of Twitter Etiquette that you should never Tweet something today that you might regret tomorrow.

Businesses also forget that they are participating in a social situation, rather than a business meeting or a conference. This can mean that they forget the most important part of a

Twitter conversation, which is engaging the general public with lively and interesting content. Businesses need to remember that their content will reflect directly upon their company or products. Constantly sticking to a business message, and even intruding into conversations with your promotions and slogans, is breaking Twitter etiquette, causing people to avoid you or even remove your comments from their page.

Breaking these simple rules of Twitter etiquette will all lead to the business's reputation being damaged, but there is another way of breaking the rules about Tweets which can cause lasting damage, and most businesses don't even realize that they are doing it. This is the boring, restricted Tweet which does not even interest people who are already following you. A dull Tweet is the worst kind of rudeness, because it implies that you cannot be bothered to create anything more interesting. It also tars your product with the same dull brush, making your promotions less desirable, and resulting in permanent damage to the business's reputation. In fact, Twitter etiquette rules are designed to ensure that account holders don't post dull Tweets and comments.

Understanding Twitter Content Etiquette

In order to create content which is memorable and that is likely to create comments, it is important to understand what Twitter etiquette has to say about content. As there is no definitive list of etiquette rules, it can be hard to define exactly what you need to do in order to create content that confirms to those requirements. However, the general consensus around Twitter content is as follows:

- **Add Value:** Never write a Tweet that is 'empty', or contains no new information. Constantly repeating the same Tweet over and over again does not add Value. Creating interesting Tweets about your business or products will.

- **Be Engaged:** Create content which is relevant to your follower's interests. Just talking about your own business is boring. Instead, engage with followers, and even help them in their businesses.

- **Mix and Match:** Create interesting content by talking about things other than the business. It is important to remember that you need to relate those Tweets to the company: keep opposing interests for a personal Twitter account.

- **Expand:** Don't limit yourself to 'yes' and 'no' Tweets, and when replying to another's comments, make sure that other followers can understand what you are replying to. You can also expand your thoughts in order to create several Tweets around a single theme.

- **Focus:** Don't let your Tweets run wild. Sticking to certain areas for your content ideas allows you to write about them more fully. Inane or shallow Tweets are likely to be dull.

- **Plan:** Don't write don't whatever you are thinking at the moment. Instead, create Tweet plans, and stick to them in order to create interesting Tweets.

- **Enjoy:** Have fun with your Tweeting. Your content is likely to be more interesting and engaging if you are enjoying writing about it. By enjoying the content, you are also more likely to produce lasting Tweets, ones that don't look dull after a day or so.

Creating Good Content

By following the rules of Twitter etiquette, you can start to create content that everyone wants to read. In order to make sure that you are always producing the best content - that is Tweets that are full of value and entertainment, you need to bear in mind some simple hints which will ensure that your content meets the standards required.

The first idea is simply to be you - to represent your business and products naturally, without any additions or falsity. Some larger businesses have damaged their reputations by failing to provide a natural account of themselves - see for example the famous Chipotle's faked hacking which gathered enormous criticism - and the result for smaller companies could be even more serious. Being able to create a natural environment for your Tweets means that business posts won't be as obvious, and you are also more likely to reach readers who are not solely interested in business or marketing. Success in Twitter is usually predicated upon being open and honest about yourself - rather than just being there to further business interests.

Another factor to be remembered is that most Twitter accounts are considered to be a representation of the company. On the internet, there is surprisingly little distance between the post and the real person, and this can mean that everything you Tweet is regarded as being emblematic of the company. Some experts consider that, on Twitter, users become what they Tweet - and reputations are made and lost through this viewpoint. Good content, therefore, needs to display the business at its best; every single time there is a Tweet.

The other important factor to remember is that Tweeting is a way of building relationships between the business and its customers. Content is there to help those relationships, and while professional and business content is important, in reality it is all about the interaction between the company and the customers. Engaging with people is an essential part of creating good content, and if you are not achieving this, then you are essentially wasting your Twitter opportunity.

Twitter account holders can use the rules of Twitter content etiquette to ensure that they reach out of the right people, and get better responses to their Tweets. Good, interesting content is all about adding value, adding interest, and providing something for your readers. By using the rules of content creation, Twitter account users can create content which avoids dull, promotion-like Tweets, and also avoid creating messages which intrude into other user's conversations. Clear, precise and accurate content will always be more interesting than anything offered by those solely dedicating themselves to business promotions, product selling, and talking about their company. By following the simple rules of Twitter etiquette, Twitter account holders can get so much more out of their Tweets, and create worthwhile, relevant content which encourages viewers to follow them and talk about them to others. By creating better content, users can ensure that their business reputation rises, and more people come to view their company as an engaging, interesting and worthwhile business.

How Tweeting Excessively Breaks the Rules of Twitter Etiquette

Twitter has become a focal point for anyone trying to promote a business, a product, or simply improve the reputation of their brand. Using Twitter can allow followers to see the human side of a business, can help develop better relationships between a company and their customers, and even extend the familiarity of the brand. However, many people come to Twitter with only a basic idea of what to do, and sometimes this inexperience shows. One of the biggest problems for people trying to market their business through Twitter is that they tend to overdo it. They Tweet excessively, becoming addicted to messaging their followers over every little thing. Despite their enthusiasm, and the fact that they are trying to link themselves to their followers, Twitter is not the place to carpet-bomb your customers with promotions and comments.

Guilty of Excessive Tweeting?

Businesses want to get their message across are often guilty of using too many Tweets in the course of a day. They might have a program which sends the same Tweet every hour, for example, but they add more to their account by retweeting other's comments. With actions like this, they can soon start cluttering up their follower's accounts, and generally make themselves hugely unwelcome. Constantly Tweeting is seen as attention-seeking, the person who always relates every conversation back to their own experiences, and if your Tweets are repetitive, then you are essentially spamming people. That is not good, and so you might need to take stock and consider whether you are guilty of excessive Tweeting. Here are some of the reasons why you might be losing followers:

- **People Regularly Unfollow You:** Losing followers is a fact of life, and it can happen to the most popular people on the planet. However, if you are losing people on a regular basis, particularly if they join and then leave after a few days, then it could be because of your excessive Tweeting. Sometimes, people will even say 'I'm leaving because you tweet too much'.

- **You Use the Same Tweet:** You've written a Tweet about your business, or perhaps about a promotion, and you want to make sure that people take note of it. So you program it into your Twitter bot, and allow it to send out the message on a repeating timeline. Soon your Twitter account looks like a looped tape, and people are completely ignoring you.

- **Your Tweets Overlap:** If you send out a Tweet, and then another Tweet, and then another, you are more likely to be over-using the Tweet button. It is a good idea to use everything in moderation, and this includes Twitter. Try to stick to only one Tweet per day or one Tweet in the morning, perhaps, and another in the afternoon if you really must.

- **You Tweet on the Wrong Day:** Evidence shows that businesses need to focus their Tweets on particular days of the week - particularly Saturday and Sunday if it wasn't completely obvious. However, most small businesses work Monday to Friday, and that is when they send out most of their Tweets. Generally, if your Tweet percentage drops during the weekend, then you are not spacing out your posts evenly, and are over-doing it during the week.

• **Your Tweets Have No Value:** The main essence of Twitter is to ensure that you communicate well with your followers, and if you are constantly sending out empty and vapid Tweets, or essentially the same message again and again, then you are breaking one of the most important rules of Twitter etiquette - always add value. If you have nothing to say, then why send out a Tweet at all?

• **You Tweet Replies to Everything:** More common among current Twitter users than previously, the Reply button has lead to a general increase in the number of Tweets produced each day. If you can't take a break because you are worried about missing a comment, then it is time to take a closer look at the message you are sending out with your excessive Tweeting.

Why You Need to Change

Although it is already clear that anyone who Tweets too much is likely to put off their followers, businesses are tempted to do it because they believe that they are 'putting the brand about', getting it out there into the general population. However, what they don't realize is that excessive amounts of Tweeting can have a detrimental effect on their sales. Recent research suggests that there is a maximum number of posts-per-day that will be tolerated, and after this the uptake and response ratio drops dramatically. Followers may even quit your account due to the number of Tweets going in. Essentially, if you are delivering more than about 4 Tweets a day (maximum), then you are likely to be losing business, and alienating people who would have otherwise have been interested in your product.

Excessive Tweeting doesn't just mean losing people that are your followers, because your account is out there in the Twitterverse, where it can be seen by those searching for your industry. So you are not only cluttering up your own and your follower's accounts, you are also affecting other businesses. Continually posting too much, and with nothing to say, can reduce your influence in the business world, and may damage your reputation in the industry. These are serious concerns which Twitter users need to consider before they press the 'send' button again.

Why Breaking Twitter Etiquette Can Damage Your Brand

Perhaps the most important lesson businesses need to learn before they start a Twitter account is that poor etiquette can easily damage the business and the reputation of the brand. Twitter is not a game, at least for those trying to make a commercial impact online, and it should not be treated lightly. There are several ways in which breaking Twitter etiquette can do real harm to your business profile.

- **Breaking Etiquette Makes You Seem Rude:** The fact is, people expect a certain level of politeness when they are reading Twitter. They don't want to be constantly bombarded by information from the same company - that is why there are anti-spam programs. If you consistently break Etiquette by Tweeting excessively, then you are essentially being rude to potential customers, which is never good business.

- **Breaking Etiquette Makes You Seem Unprofessional:** For the same reasons described above, excessive Tweeting is sign of a business which is not professional, and that is likely to put people off.

- **Breaking Etiquette Undermines the Brand:** If you set up an account on Twitter in order to engage with the general public and improve the brands image, then excessive Tweeting is the worst thing you could do. It will make the rudeness and unprofessional approach of the Tweets seem like part of the brand, tarnishing the reputation.

- **Breaking Etiquette Could Get You Banned:** Like most other social networking sites, Twitter wants to reduce the amount of spam its users produce. If you are constantly sending out the same robotic message, interfering with other people's use of the network, then your account could easily be suspended.

- **Breaking Etiquette Fails to Engage:** For all of the reasons above, if you Tweet excessively, then you are effectively reducing the impact of your messages to your followers. Instead, you are most likely to drive them away, meaning they are unlikely to connect with your business, and unlikely to buy your brand.

Making sure that you follow the rules of Twitter by not sending too many messages will make sense to the businessman or marketer who genuinely wants to engage with their customers. Breaking the Etiquette means that you are reducing your chances of finding out what customers want, or discovering what they like or dislike about the brand. The etiquette rules are designed to help people manage their accounts effectively, and Businesses can turn it into a positive, using it to reach out to potential customers and enhance their brand.

The mistake of excessive Tweeting is one which many businesses are prone to, because they believe that they are interacting with their customers. Once they understand that it is a mistake, and they are driving away the very people they want to engage, most companies reduce their Tweet count, and start communicating properly. With the rise of the 'conversation', connected Tweets between followers, it is all too easy to let the Tweet count get on top of you. In order to avoid this completely, companies need to take control of the amount of Tweets they deliver each day, including replies and Tweets which promote the business. If you are reluctant to let go of the marketing Tweet completely, confine it to once a day, including weekends, or consider adding Hashtags which connect to relevant aspects of your business.. On the whole, however, it is much better to try and reduce the overall number of Tweets in a week, concentrating instead on producing more focused, precise and relevant posts.

Get the Best from Conversations Using the Rules of Twitter Etiquette

Conversations are the key to communication in Twitter, and they are essential to anyone who wants to make an impression in this social media network. In addition to being helpful to business and commercial interests, they are also being used by medical researchers and journalists. The interest which a Twitter conversation arouses can be used to promote products, increase the reputation of a brand, or simply to personalize a company. Creating Twitter conversations should be one of the key focuses of a marketing expert, and in order to get the best from this simple device, it is important to understand what it is, how it functions, and how using the right Twitter etiquette can make a great deal of difference.

What are Twitter Conversations?

Twitter conversations are communications between account holders, usually keeping to a single topic or referring back to that topic when inviting others into a conversation. Unlike Tweets, which are posted by the same person and can be completely unconnected, conversations are interactions between different people. In addition, they also allow people to extend their Tweets beyond the 140 character restrictions by posting in a 'conversation' style. Recent additions have also allowed people to catch up with a conversation easily using the blue line. Most experts agree that Twitter conversations are as important as Hashtags for spreading a company's message or generating interest in the business. For example, when promoting a brand or product, a simple Tweet can become a conversation by having followers comment on the promotion. Others will reply to that comment, and so a Twitter conversation is started. Of course, most Tweets don't get this kind of attention, and only occasionally will a promotion about a particular product result in a conversation. It might be tempting to try and start a conversation about the promotion by asking questions, or intruding into other people's conversations, but it is just not this easy to generate a natural, spontaneous discussion about your business or product.

Natural conversations are the key to getting the best out of a Twitter account, as forced discussions, or excessive promotions, will break the rules of Twitter etiquette, and may cause your Tweets to be ignored, or even result in your account being removed. Even if these consequences don't happen, pushing your promotions forward like this, in an obvious manner, will still give your brand and business a negative reputation. Your account will seem rather like the unwelcome person at a party, who repeatedly barges into conversations in a loud and intimidating manner, and who is generally shunned and avoided as a consequence. In order to avoid your Twitter conversations ending up in rejection, clever marketers need to develop subtle ways to encourage followers and passersby to talk about their products. Being able to follow conversations on relevant topics, and contribute to these discussions is one way to make sure that you are not unwelcome. There are several devices designed to help marketing experts keep track of relevant Tweets, mostly through the use of Hashtags. This is great where users regularly use Hashtags, but for those conversations without tags, it might be necessary to use scans which specify a particular subject instead.

Understanding Conversations and Etiquette

There are several different ways to develop a conversation, and there are also different ways of joining a conversation.

This is where understanding the rules of Twitter etiquette can make a difference, as you need to know how to approach people in the right way, and how to join conversations between strangers without seeming rude. The first step in using conversations is to understand the difference between semi-private talk between friends, and more commercial talk which is available to anyone. Consider these different conversations as though this were a real-time party. You would not join in a group of friends talking about personal matters - in fact, it would not even be polite to listen in. On the other hand, you might be encouraged or even expected to join in conversations about business matters, or other discussions where you could contribute.

The other aspect to politeness over conversations is to make sure that you join in. Most small business owners join Twitter in a wave of enthusiasm, and then make no comments, and even stop adding Tweets to their account. Worse, they might make occasional Tweets about their work, or about topical matters, but they don't join in conversations and they even ignore people trying to talk to them. This is not only a Twitter etiquette breach, but also a simple social failure. How do businesses reach out to people if they are not even willing to talk to them on social networks?

In order to join in a conversation, start by searching for topics relevant to your business, or to your particular interests. You will see that most are connected to other Twitter users through the @reply code. This is the best way to start talking to someone that you are not yet following. You can also use this code to include comments about other people, just as you might share something at a party. It is also a good way of joining a conversation without seeming pushy or rude. It can work very effectively as a way to start bringing a brand to the attention of people who do not usually follow you, and it is also a good way of introducing yourself to a group with similar interests to your own. The most important thing to remember is that conversations take time to get going, and so the business promoter will need to be patient.

Get the Conversations Flowing

Conversations are becoming the best way to promote products and increase the profile and reputation of a business. However, it is important to remember that not everyone comes to the networking site to talk business. Constantly intruding on their accounts with attempts to 'start' a conversation about your products (perhaps through using quizzes, or by asking direct questions associated with the promotion) is likely to make them Unfollow you, and is also likely to diminish the brand's image. Joining a conversation and adding Hashtags to the end of your Tweet will also make people stop reading your messages. These approaches consistently break the etiquette rules which govern the way in which conversations should occur.

As an alternative to this, there are several things that you can do which are completely within the rules of Twitter, but which will help with promoting the business, but will also not intrude into comments. The first, and most simple thing that you can do, is to have your account name as your business name, or some specific product which you are promoting. Joining in conversations will allow you to speak solely about the topic at hand, but will also allow you to promote your business without intruding.

Starting up conversations can be more difficult than joining one which is already in progress. It is possible to create Tweets which encourage people to participate, but these should not be solely focused upon the business. The most important thing to remember when trying to develop a conversation is that you need to give followers and viewers a reason to reply and contribute. Writing a Tweet about something relevant, eye-catching or which is always a source of debate can help to encourage people to participate. When creating these Tweets, it is important to remember that you should not write anything which would be controversial, or which has extreme opinions. Even big businesses have come under fire for Tweets which attracted negative responses, so small companies and marketers need to walk a fine line between the interesting and the excessively controversial.

A good place to start when building conversations is to have a focus. Random Tweeting can make conversations less likely. It can also mean that account holders are easily side-tracked, losing the aim of the conversation and failing to build any meaningful relationships for the business. If you set up a Tweet to discuss a particular matter - perhaps the economy, perhaps celebrities moving into business, for example - then you need to continue talking along those lines for the rest of the conversation. It is all too easy to get lost in the conversation, and start talking about your last restaurant meal, or the latest sporting results, but these will not help you gain followers who are interested in your business. It would be foolish, for example, for a romantic novelist, keen to promote her latest book, to reply to conversations about football results, or weight training. Not only would those Tweets be unwelcome to that community (for both males and females), but the novelist is also likely to estrange followers who were interested in the novels. This is another element of Twitter etiquette, where keeping to a topic, and not joining in on random conversations, ensures that you do not isolate your customer base or undermine their interested in your business.

How Twitter Etiquette Can Make or Break Your Profile

When setting up a Twitter account, one of the most important elements is the profile. Along with the right kind of content, and a good understanding of Twitter Etiquette when it comes to writing Tweets, the profile can influence how people view you when they land on your Twitter feed. This is the point where your audience meets you properly for the first time, and is in essence like being introduced to a stranger. If you want to do business with them, you will want to make a good impression from the outset, and the Twitter profile is there to ensure that your first impression is a memorable one. However, without the right kind of business profile, you may find yourself losing as many followers as you gain through good content and good manners.

Good Profiles, Bad Profiles

So what makes a good or bad Twitter profile? The key to creating the best profile possible is to use the rules of Twitter etiquette to guide you when setting up your account. Firstly, you will need to avoid any kind of innuendo or crudity. This should go without saying, but you would be surprised by the number of people who put in a name without realizing that the initials make a rude word, or the username is something negative to some. If you are setting up a business account, then your username needs to be as close as possible to your business name - @JoeBloggsWheels for example. There are also some other tips you can use to make sure that you don't blunder into a bad Twitter profile.

- **No Begging, No Pleading:** A common business mistake is to fill the profile full of the Twitter equivalent of begging letters. Writing "Follow me!" in big letters on the Twitter Feed page is pretty certainly going to put some people off. It is also going to make your brand seem desperate and unattractive.

- **No Direct Promotions:** In addition to begging and pleading, direct promotions are another big problem on Twitter. Don't try and persuade people to buy your products on the account page itself. You might include promotions in your Tweets, but the profile can do without them.

- **No Funny Remarks:** While you might think that you are the funniest person in business, your off-the-cuff joke might seem a little bit passé, dull or unfunny two or three months down the line. Quick jokes in the Tweets are fine, as long as they are good jokes, but are best left out of the profile itself.

- **No Cutesy Pictures:** No pictures of anything except images relating to the business or the brand. @RainbowChocolates can have a rainbow. @JoeBloggsWheels cannot.

There are also other things to avoid when it comes to creating your Twitter profile. What you do need to do is make sure that you fill out your landing page as effectively as possible. No-one wants to go to a Twitter account page and find that there is nothing there, just a name at the top and tumbleweed rolling past the bio page, and the account just the basic one supplied by Twitter. Most people about to become followers expect a little bit more than just the average profile. Create an impression by setting up and then maintaining your profile as you continue to Tweet.

Profiles and Twitter Etiquette

The same issues that surround the use of content and style when writing Tweets also have a considerable effect on your profile. In order to create the perfect landing page, you need to set up a clear, precise username which reflects your brand. You should also include this username in other social media sites, such as Facebook and LinkedIn. Your images should also be uniform across all these social platforms, so followers can find you easily no matter where you are writing. Etiquette requires that your name should be something which clearly links you to your business, so don't choose a name which is not memorable.

Your Bio should also be filled in, and contain information about the brand which is easy to remember, and that other users might connect with. Don't use the Bio to write a promotion for the brand, for products, or for the business. It might even be a good idea to write the Bio of the person Tweeting on behalf of the brand, telling people about what they do, and why they are on Twitter promotion the business.

Another element of Etiquette which might make or break your profile is whether you choose to protect it. Many businesses do protect, because they are concerned about hacking, and having their Twitter feed disrupted by someone changing their profile. However, when you choose to protect your Twitter feed, you are effectively blocking people from joining, making following your business or brand a chore. Making everything private has the same effect. Twitter etiquette requires politeness and the ability to interact with strangers, but by protecting your profile you are representing the brand as anti-social and even elitist. This will not be welcomed by anyone.

Starting the Twitter Profile

The essence of a Twitter profile is to represent you in as positive a light as possible. When you are writing Tweets as part of a marketing campaign for a business, your profile is also emblematic of the business, and of the brand. Therefore, a good profile should be a must-have for every Twitter marketer, and it should be the focus of your efforts during the first few days of setting up an account with the site. Even before you have a Twitter page of your own to build and improve, you need to make a start on your profile by creating a username which tells people about the business without becoming a spam slogan. The Username should be one which represents the brand, and emphasizes its identity (you do have a brand identity - right?). It has to send the right message to your followers, so don't sign up to Twitter until you have the perfect name. Here Twitter Etiquette requires that the username be open and easy to remember, so that people can find their way back to your page. The key to remember is the obligation to be engaging.

Secondly, you need to create a page which echoes your username by creating a uniform account page. This is best done in the brand's colors, perhaps with the logo as a centerpiece though this doesn't have to be so. A custom background is in keeping with the Twitter etiquette requirement that you show interest in your followers. You want to be able to show business details or allow contact information to be displayed? There's a custom background that can meet your needs. If you can't even be bothered to create a good background, you are likely to lose followers.

Next, you want to write a biography which is to the point, but also interesting. This is a good place to put the brand's interests, including music, design or IT. Make the brand live a little. Here, Twitter etiquette will favor the brand that is expansive without writing a sales brochure. This is the perfect place to locate a website URL. Clarity and good content here will win the day, while a rambling, self-obsessed bio will be rejected.

Lastly, choose a good image. Since you are promoting a business here, it doesn't have to be a photograph of the person writing the Tweets. What it does have to be is relevant, with a clear connection between the main brand and the picture. Twitter etiquette frowns upon unconnected Tweets, and the same will be true of an unrelated or false image as your profile picture. Complement the image by creating an attractive background for your feed, and set up a header image which is either a smaller copy of the main picture, or which, again, reflects that image. A good picture can make a Twitter profile, while a bad one, which breaks Twitter etiquette, is likely to lose followers.

Profiles and Etiquette

When it comes to creating the perfect profile, Twitter users have to have one eye on the rules of etiquette which govern behavior on the site. Remember that you are creating a landing page to engage your customers. If you concentrate upon promoting the brand, to the detriment of your profile, then Twitter will find you out. Rule breakers will find it harder to generate followers, and are more likely to lose the interest of those who would otherwise have followed their feed.

Learning and understanding the rules of etiquette as it relates to the Twitter profile can save business marketers a lot of time and effort. Set up the account right in the first place, and you are more likely to see rewards in the form of more visitors, and greater acceptance from people your brand would like to follow. A good profile, accompanied by worthwhile Tweets, will ensure that your business campaign is a success.

When Shameless Self-Promotion Breaks All the Rules of Twitter Etiquette

Businesses join Twitter in order to promote themselves to interested followers, and to generate conversation about promotions, products or their brand. However, there is a point where being keen about a product crosses the line into self-promotion, and this can cause a lot of damage to the reputation of a company. It is sometimes a little hard to decide exactly where the moment comes, but businesses can easily move from being popular to being the 'Most Unfollowed Account of the day'. Shameless self-promotion is the key to getting yourself a bad reputation, and will also but the brakes on any kind of close communication between the Twitter feed and your followers.

What Counts As Shameless Self Promotion

Twitter is a great place to promote your latest brand, product or money-off promotion, but it can also be a place where shameless self-promotion flourishes. In order to understand the difference between promoting yourself, and being completely shameless about it, businesses need to look at who they are talking to, how they are talking, and why they are doing it. All too often, a little bit of harmless promotion can become intrusive and obnoxious, sometimes without the marketer running the account even realizing. The art of promoting yourself on Twitter needs to be subtle, and anything else is clearly shameless.

- **Only Talking Promotions:** One of the most common mistakes of those new to Twitter is the promotional Tweet. Constantly repeating information

82

about the promotion, ignoring anything which isn't directly related to it, and offering nothing new, just re-warming yesterday's nearly identical Tweet, are all signs that the business is now shamelessly self-promoting.

• **Direct Messaging to Talk about the Business:** DM is not designed to be a vehicle for a business to talk to its followers about promotions or products. If you are sending out automated direct messages, particularly if these contain sales copy, you are most likely spamming your followers. You are also likely to be losing those followers at an ever increasing rate.

• **Adding a Promotion at the Bottom of a Tweet:** Even if the content you have written has nothing whatsoever to do with the business, putting a Hashtag at the bottom involving the product, a promotion or anything related to the company is definitely shameless self-promotion, and should be avoided. Senseless Tweeting like this will get your Twitter account a bad name, and will have a negative effect on your brand's reputation.

• **Creating Quizzes or Polls Which Only Promotes the Business:** Creating quizzes is a popular method of finding out how your followers feel about your brand. However, if your quiz is simply designed to promote your product, then you are promoting yourself at the expense of connecting with your followers. Twitter isn't the inventor of this promotional style- many brands have used this Quiz-style device in magazines for years. However, they at least had the sense to place an 'advertisement' sign at the top of the page.

- **Joining Business Conversations and then Promoting Your Company:** Sometimes it is ok in business chat to include your company in Hashtags at the bottom of the comment. However, if you are hunting out businesses and their conversations in order to make that Tweet, you are self-promoting to unbearable levels.

- **Joining any Conversation and then Promoting the Company:** As above, only much worse, hijacking a conversation and adding an irrelevant Tweet about your business is not only shamelessly self-promoting, it is also likely to get you suspended from Twitter. That kind of behavior is considered to be spam, and you could even be suspended from it.

Self-Promotion and Twitter Etiquette

Like most social media networks, Twitter is able to comfortably accommodate most business accounts, and can put up with a lot of selling and brand-building on the site. Twitter etiquette, the unwritten rules which govern what you can and cannot do and say with your account, have been developed so that business users can get a good idea of what they are and are not allowed to say. For example, etiquette offers guidelines about the level of promotion, and tends to emphasize communication and interaction, rather than simply plugging away with your sales copy. So when Twitter users start to move from talking about their business occasionally to promoting it more vigorously, it makes sense for them to understand exactly where the lines are being drawn.

Firstly, it is perfectly acceptable to build a Twitter account based around a brand. Most big businesses have settled into Twitter, and they have a solid fan base of readers who like to talk to the big companies. However, it is important not to overstep the mark when building the account. For example, you should not use promotional 'SALE' signs as your Twitter picture, background or header image. You should also not write your bio as though it were a flyer for your business.

Secondly, business Tweets are also accepted on the site, although there needs to be a level of moderation here in order to avoid becoming shameless. Your Twitter feed needs to be a mix of promotional material, talking about business news and articles, and other relevant information. None of the latter types of post should have a Hashtag at the bottom with your brand or product in the link. Tweeting is much easier after you have a few followers, since you can start to focus on what interests them outside your company. Being able to engage with your clients is a big part of keeping up with Twitter etiquette.

Thirdly, you can find out about similar businesses that are also members of Twitter, and have conversations with them about your company, or the industry, or anything else which is relevant. The occasional promotion here is perfectly in line with Twitter etiquette. However, you must resist attacking rivals here, either mocking them or claiming to be better than them. Your followers won't like it, and you could end up accidently promoting your rivals while blackening your own image.

Avoiding Self Promotion

Business Twitter users tend to focus upon their company, and this can be a vulnerability which makes them promote themselves in a way which is not acceptable to the rest of the Twitter community. Of course, businesses create an account in order to Tweet about themselves, but it should not be the main conversation in their Twitter feed. If every single Tweet concerns the business, the brand or a product, then you are not really fulfilling your purpose in joining the site. Businesses should remember that each Tweet is a communication between themselves and their followers, potential customers. You couldn't corner a stranger at a party and heckle them with sales copy and promotions, and it should be the same principle on Twitter. Avoiding self-promotion doesn't mean completely neglecting the business side of you, but it does mean allowing it to take second place to affective and expansive social networking.

The best thing that users can do is to commit themselves to engaging with people on Twitter in a social way. You can talk to them about anything you like, as long as the business purpose is kept to a minimum. They might want to talk about a product, or ask you questions about it, and here you can show your commitment to them by replying, or providing them with useful information. Building a following by reducing the amount of business tweets will be more effective than just pumping out promotional links and Hashtags as though you had forgotten that you did that yesterday - or this morning - or an hour ago.

Avoiding self-promotion also means making a commitment to the long-term possibilities which Twitter opens up. Being there on the site is not just about making an impact for the newest part of your company. Instead, it is about building brand awareness. You can do this through your Twitter account name, and through the images you use on your profile page. What you should avoid is repetitively linking to your business website, or mentioning it on every Tweet. By providing a more rounded image of your business, you will be able to create interest in the brand without having to force it into every conversation.

Careful planning is the key to promoting your business in a Twitter-friendly way. Lay out exactly what you want to achieve by joining Twitter, whether that is greater brand awareness, an increase in sales, or the desire to improve the reputation of the business by interacting with customers. Once you have your key focus, you can then put this in to practice through your Twitter account. Build your brand through the company profile. Increase sales by joining industry conversations and providing thoughtful and insightful comments which will give your products distinct personality, and improve the reputation of the business through direct communication with followers. Encourage customers to follow you by providing your username with your sales invoice. Remember to keep the balance between promotion and communication, and you should see the benefits with increased follower numbers, and a more positive reception for future Tweets.

The Twitter Style Rules That Can Save your Reputation

Businesses are turning to Twitter as a way to introduce their brand to the general public. However, because they fail to understand the implications of each Tweet, and the fact that mistakes can seriously damage their reputation, many businesses are suffering as a result of joining the social networking site. The problem is that most Twitter users just don't understand the style rules which govern how Tweets should be formed, and the content they should contain. The fact that they don't understand this can result in poor reception from other users, and may result in an account which is not followed, and a brand which is considered to be pointless or worthless. Before a business even opens up a Twitter account, the marketing sector needs to fully understand what it means to participate in Twitter, and how the right use of Style can help them to save the reputation of their company, and their brand.

What is Twitter Style?

Some marketers or business owners might be familiar with the style rules for essay writing, used by different universities and colleges. What they may not realize is that there is also a system of rules for writing styles in Twitter. The majority of Twitter account users don't follow these style guidelines, which is why there are so many Tweets which essentially say "omg. R U #having #a #laugh". This basic Twitter style is easy to write, but it can be hard for followers to read, and it also has very little actually content. Readers who expect more from their messages are going to be disappointed.

Twitter style divides the Tweet up into several standard forms, including those which provide mentions to other contributors through the @ format, the reply (which has the @reply format) and Acknowledgements (using /cc to signify who the Tweet is aimed at). Tagging and Retweets are also essential style skills which any business leader has to understand before they start their Twitter account. To ensure that you use the correct style for the correct type of message, businesses should make a list defining each step, like this:

- **Formal Mentions:** if you want to include the name of a company or a person already on Twitter, then you can achieve this easily using the @accountname format. Your message will then be linked to the named Twitter account. They will be aware that you have mentioned them, and you might also get a response from them. You can also add the name in this format: @Joe Bloggs (JoeBloggs14). When writing out a Tweet, it is important to add comment before the name, unless the Tweet is part of a conversation. Creating a separate Tweet with the formal mention first will prevent your other followers from seeing it.

- **The Reply:** For a more direct message to another Twitter user, the Reply is essential. There is standard formatting for this type of message, and any change to that format could leave the reply in limbo. Now that Twitter uses 'conversations' this is particularly important.

- **The Acknowledgement:** More than just the direct reply, this is often used when passing on content from another user. These comments should be after the content, and include a message to indicate that the person

89

being thanked is the originator of the content. Failure to acknowledge correctly will create resentment and hostility.

• **ReTweets:** Like acknowledgements, this Tweet will include content from another user. The main aim of the ReTweet is to pass information among your followers. There is a formula designed to help people acknowledge retweets, including the letters RT, and then adding the account name of the original Tweet's writer. Fortunately, most modern social media clients allow users to retweet directly onto their account page, formatting the style automatically.

Using these style rules will help you to define the content of your Tweet, but it will not help you in setting out the rest of that content. Although you will have correctly replied to someone, or retweeted in the right manner, if the rest of the content is poor, you will not have achieved anything. In order to understand how to get the most from your Tweets, you also need to follow the general style rules for every Tweet.

General Style Rules

There is more to the rules of Tweet style than just these basic formulas. Once you have created a reply or an acknowledgement, then you will need to fill in the rest of the content yourself, and this is where mistakes can be made. The main problem with the Twitter system is that it restricts users to a platform of just 140 characters per Tweet. This is not a great deal, and has led to a lot of abbreviation, the use of programs designed to shorten your writing to fit into the character limit, and sloppy writing which relies upon links to other Twitter accounts in order to get its message across. Rather than go down this route, following some basic Twitter style advice can really help you to achieve what you want without damaging your reputation.

- **Never Abbreviate:** With so little space, abbreviation is a big temptation for most Twitter users. However, when you shorten words, or use letters to stand for words, you can make yourself seem unprofessional, and even idiotic. It also reduces the impact of your Tweets, turning them into vapid, teenage comments that most of your followers would avoid.

- **Never Over-Tweet:** Another option for writing everything you need to is to use combination Tweets. Although many users are choosing to go for this option now, creating 'conversations' which link six or seven tweets together, this is a big mistake. Rather than doing this, it makes sense to write a blog post containing all of your idea, and then link to this through Twitter.

- **Never Use Only URLs:** While linking to blogs can be ideal, a single URL on its own is poor Twitter etiquette, and won't receive the clicks that you require. Instead, always make sure that you include content before the link is added.

- **Never Ignore your Followers:** Perhaps the single biggest mistake made by businesses using Twitter for commercial reasons is ignoring the followers they gain. Companies have discovered that Twitter is a great way to connect with their fans, but they should remember to pay attention to what their followers want - this includes the content they submit, and the links that are included in Tweets.

• **Avoid Robot Tweets:** Another common error made by commercial Twitter users is to have some of their work created by robots. These programs are supposed to help businesses create Tweets easily, but they can easily turn into spamming programs that produce irrelevant and inane content which is obviously created without care or consideration. Followers can quickly drop out of sight if businesses rely upon robots to create their Twitter feed.

While the basic rules of style for Twitter might seem obvious, there are still many companies out there making the mistake of not correctly formatting and styling their content. The lack of correct formula can easily make their products seem less attractive, and followers could be put off of buying items from a company with poorly-written Tweets. These style guidelines are just a hint to how to put your content together. What is important is that Tweet writers should consider their content as an essential communication tool.

When writing or preparing a Tweet for your business account, writers should pay attention to the content, and to the message that it is conveying about the company and the brand. Well-written content is likely to reveal a brand that cares about its users, and that is likely to produce more sales, and a better brand image. Poorly written content, particularly Tweets which are produced by software programs, are likely to create a poor brand perception among other Twitter users.

It is not necessary to obey all of these Twitter rules all of the time, but when you are writing for business, it makes sense to adopt a professional attitude towards the Twitter account. Don't view it as a sideline, or a chore, but instead put effort into creating an attractive, well-designed Twitter feed. Using the correct type of style will help you to format your Tweets so that they are relevant to your business. Think of it as writing a portfolio of your business interests. You would not abbreviate words, or create links without explanation in a written document, and it is important to take those principles with you when creating the Twitter account. Using these style formulas will help you to ensure that you get your message across clearly, succinctly, and in a way that will allow other users to copy your Tweets and send them to their friends and family. It is also likely to help you to generate comment which will improve your business reputation, and ensure that followers view your brand as worthwhile and relevant to their own interests.

Cut Back on Marketing Keywords to Improve your Twitter Etiquette

Twitter recently updated the process which allows business Twitter users to market themselves using keywords. One of the main purposes of creating an account tends to be using Tweets to advertise a business, but this has both pros and cons which can affect how people view the business, and how they respond to advertising from them. Using Promoted Tweets, which are a form of advertising, business users can now direct their marketing towards a particular section of their followers, or even towards a particular user. This means that followers will see promotional Tweets which relate directly to their interests. However, for the majority of Twitter followers, the social networking site is not a big advertising billboard, and they tend to be annoyed and frustrated by businesses attempting to market their products to them in the guise of Tweeting.

There has been an increase in the number of businesses using keywords to directly target Twitter users, but for the company that is hoping to build a lasting relationship with their followers, one which includes conversations, communication and engaging contact, keyword marketing could be a big step backwards, and may even be a serious mistake by the business. Although these keywords are supposed to be driven by follower interest, in most cases they are likely to cause a drop-off in replies, less conversations, and the eventual loss of followers.

What are Twitter Marketing Keywords?

Keywords can be used in Twitter to drive people towards your feed. These keywords are often chosen using Google tools which allow you to find trending words from searches on that site, but they can also be taken directly from Twitter by looking at the 'trending topics' list available to users of that site. These keywords are then placed into Tweets, either directly into the content, or by attaching them as Hashtags at the bottom of the comment. The keywords are meant to bring in more viewers, attract comment, and also encourage your usual followers to view and comment on your Tweet.

The downside to keyword marketing on Twitter is that it is difficult to write a short, 140 character post which includes one or more keywords in a natural and subtle way. Most often the sentence is just interrupted by the keyword, like a foghorn, and distracts the reader. They may also be shoehorned into the end or irrelevant comments through the use of Hashtags, and again this is disturbing to the reader and looks considerably less than natural. Using marketing keywords like this breaks a good number of the rules of Twitter etiquette, and can also mean that the business looks like a sales site, something that most savvy Twitter users will be keen to avoid.

How Using Keywords Disrupts Your Twitter Feed

Comments on Twitter are set into a profile, and the latest Tweets appear on the Twitter feed. In most profiles, there is a natural progression from talking about one subject, to discussing another. It might only be an account of eating breakfast, followed by a picture of Lunch, but there is relevance and interest there. A business profile is slightly different, but the feed should still flow naturally, as one conversation leads to comments about a business article, or a promotion leads to a debate about the use of the product. Using marketing keywords affects how this feed looks to viewers, particularly over a few days or weeks. While a daily Tweet using a keyword might not seem much, when a reader can see a whole week's worth of comment, with a keyword in use on each Tweet, it looks very obvious.

Using Marketing keywords like this breaks one of the rules of Twitter etiquette, which is not promoting the business in too blatant a fashion. When using keywords to target specific groups of followers, or those who are yet to join your feed, this is clearly self-promotion, and it can be easily spotted by most viewers. Unlike in the early years of social media, when keywords could be attached to Facebook posts or YouTube comments, and they were acceptable, the modern audience for marketers is much more sophisticated, and is likely to reject posts which too openly use keywords as a marketing tactic.

In addition, using keywords can disrupt your Twitter feed because they make the business writer change their Tweets, and this can result in an unnatural feed. Excessive amounts of keywords can even make your followers conclude that you are a 'bot', programmed to write content on keywords. An occasional use of a keyword can have a positive effect, but once it starts affecting how you write your Twitter content, it will also start having a negative impact on those reading your posts.

Twitter Etiquette and Keywords

Although the people at the top of the Twitter pyramid might be developing ways for users to do more with keywords, the feeling among the general public, the average Twitter user, is rather different. Most dislike the impact which keywords have on Tweets, and particularly those which involve the use of Hashtags as a way of introducing a sales pitch into the conversation. Twitter etiquette has long considered the overuse of these tools as poor business practice, since it tends to alienate followers, the very group of people that business Twitter users are trying to reach.

Concentrating upon keywords also breaks the rules which encourage a more natural style of communication with your Twitter followers. The rules encourage manual creation of posts because it has a better feel, and is more likely to generate a response. However, if you are manually typing in keywords, then you may lose whatever impact the natural style created.

Using keywords can also have a negative effect on the general content of your Tweets. If you are striving to put in as many keywords as possible, or trying to produce a keyword-containing Tweet from out of nowhere, then you are likely to find that your content deteriorates. From creating attractive and relevant content, you might discover that your Tweets are now all about the keyword, and this has moved the focus of your account from gentle business promotion into something which does not answer the needs of your followers. Again, this breaks Twitter etiquette rules by failing to take into account the needs of those who follow your Tweets, and by failing to engage your followers through the use of interesting and non-promotional Tweets.

In addition, the use of keywords in place of good content is seen as generally rude and anti-social. Keywords oblige you to create Tweets which are focused upon that word, rather than on your followers, on articles which might interest them, or on conversations on your Twitter feed. This is essentially putting your business needs before the Twitter community, and this is frowned upon in the rules of Twitter etiquette.

Are Any Keywords Acceptable?

The problem with using any kind of keyword, as noted above, is that it is unnatural. Keywords don't appear in social conversation, and so they should not really appear in Twitter feeds. However, this doesn't mean that there is no role for keywords in Twitter. The fact that it has been made easier to use marketing keywords suggests that the Twitter managers understand that businesses are crying out for ways to use their traditional tool in Tweets. However, they have also organized Twitter so that intrusive or hijacking keywords are prohibited. Managing the two elements is therefore tricky for the small business, or for the marketing entrepreneur.

Deciding whether any kind of marketing keywords is acceptable is chiefly a matter of personal choice. The business must weigh up the different elements involved in the debate, considering whether they need keywords to promote the brand to the right section of the public, or whether it would alienate the followers that they already have. When making this decision, the impact of Twitter etiquette must not be forgotten. Although these are unwritten rules, and therefore are only guidelines, most Twitter users do expect to see account holders following these rules. Anyone who breaks Twitter etiquette, either through using too many keywords, not adding any other kind of content, or simply talking too much about their business, is likely to suffer the consequences, including rejection, loss of followers, and being ignored by the community as a whole.

Keywords have been a staple of business promotion for many years now, and most internet users are accustomed to seeing them in web pages, articles and even some social media sites. However, with the ever-changing landscape of business communication, there is now less need to directly marketing your brand through keywords, and more emphasis upon communicating with interested parties to create a relationship. If you are using marketing keywords on Twitter, and breaking the etiquette rules that bind users of that site, then it is really a question of whether you are achieving modern business goals, or if you are falling back into a traditional position which will only alienate you from potential customers, damaging your brand in the process.

Use Twitter Etiquette to Guide Your Marketing Campaigns

Running a marketing campaign on Twitter should be easy. The social media network allows businesses to reach out to potential customers all over the world, and it also offers the space to present a positive image of the brand to the general public. However, correctly promoting a business through Twitter is not always as easy as it might seem. Many small companies find that their Twitter marketing campaigns falls flat, and there is a general lack of interest in anything they might be selling. They tend to struggle to find the right tone, and the right followers, to create a buzz around their company, and this means that their brand doesn't get the recognition they wanted. The fact is that marketing to Twitter without understanding the rules and processes can leave companies struggling in the dust, and unless the marketing manager knows what they are doing when they take on Twitter, the brand could be ignored, or develop a bad reputation for being empty and dull.

The right way to approach a marketing campaign on Twitter involves carefully planning the campaign to focus upon a particular target audience, and to bring out the best in the brand. Being able to concentrate upon the brand without creating spam is a difficult balance to walk, and unless the marketing departments feel confident that they can toe that line, and then any effort on Twitter might be wasted. Knowing and understanding your social media platform can help you to create a better marketing campaign, and one of the chief elements of Twitter is that its unwritten etiquette rules can actually help marketers to generate more interest and get better results from their Tweets.

Twitter Etiquette and Marketing

The etiquette of social media networks is sometimes abandoned when businesses seek to promote a new brand to the general public. They may consider that simply putting the brand logo and design out there, with no further effort, is all they need to do in order to create interest. However, unlike most marketing areas, where a campaign can be implemented overnight and posters or fliers distributed the next day, Twitter marketing requires commitment and long-term vision. In these circumstances, people can find it hard to find the time to work on their Twitter etiquette. In ignoring the general rules of politeness, they are missing an important step in creating the perfect image for their brand. In order to understand how using etiquette can improve your business reputation, it is first essential to learn how the wrong moves can have a negative effect.

Firstly, many businesses choose to use computer programs, known as 'bots' which are designed to regularize the Tweets and create a focused and uniform content for your account. While it is great to be focused, and important to have a clear content aim, employing bots to do this type of work is completely against the rules of Twitter etiquette. In most cases, followers might join up quickly to see what the big fuss is about, but they will soon unfollow your account once they discover the rigid content of your Tweets. It is much better to hand-write your content, in order to give it an authentic and natural flavor which will bring in lasting followers.

It is also a bad idea to use tricks and bought-follower schemes. Just to start with, it is likely to get you thrown out of the network. Twitter can not only expel you from one account, they can also block your internet address, meaning that the business will not be able to join again. Although companies might be tempted to improve their ranking by purchasing followers, in the long term it is a mistake. Not only that, but once fans of the brand discover that you have been buying in support (and they will find out, that is just how the internet works), they are likely to abandon the brand and give you a broadside into the bargain. Buying in followers is one way to ruin your brand's reputation for good.

Since you are clearly going to have to write your own content and get real followers, you need to concentrate upon the content of your Tweets. In the world of the 'net, content really is King, and you should make as much effort as possible in order to ensure that your followers get something real from your Tweets. Experts describe worthwhile Tweets as 'adding value', which means that they contain information, comment or insight that your followers cannot get from anywhere else. If your Tweet's don't add value to your followers, the business is not going to be popular, and could struggle to hold on to the followers that it does have.

While you are writing out this important content, it is also vital that you make this content as natural as possible. Businesses often make the mistake of thinking that Tweets have to be like website pages: i.e. full of keywords and SEO designed to bring customers to your website. But if you constantly stuff your Tweets with keywords (and remember that you only have 140 characters per Tweet), then you are likely to sound automated and uninventive. Worse, you could be boring your poor followers to tears with an unrelenting stream of keywords and links to your website, and this is likely to drive them into the arms of another Twitter feed.

Another issue with content is the use of Hashtags. These can be essential in helping to monitor conversation, since search tools will look for followers using these tags. However, it is all too easy to break the rules of Twitter etiquette by over-using Hashtags, or hijacking an unconnected conversation with Hashtags concerning your business. There are so many Hashtag rules that it can be hard to avoid breaking some of them, but if you can keep within the rules of Hashtag use, then you will ensure a better reputation for your business.

Even if you manage to avoid all of the pitfalls described above, there is still a danger that you might not be attracting people to your Twitter feed. The most common problem is simply the content of your Tweets. If you have a feed which basically reads as one long promotion for the brand, or is simply filled with facts about the business, then you will not get the followers you need. Instead, you should be creating content which has a fine balance of information about the brand, discussion on topical issues, and thoughts about personal matters which relate to the writer, rather than the business.

Using Etiquette to your Advantage

Once you understand these rules, and are certain that you can avoid the pitfalls of running a marketing campaign in this platform, you might find that Twitter etiquette can actually help you to get more from your campaign. The basic rules of politeness can ensure that you get more followers than you expected, and could generate interest in your brand. There are a few steps to using Twitter etiquette to guide you:

1.   **Give your Followers Respect:** Once you have gained followers, don't ignore them in order to concentrate upon winning over new ones. Treat your followers as you would real-time friends, by talking to them about their interests, and paying attention to their opinions on the brand. You should also take care not to spam followers' message boxes, as this is likely to make your hemorrhage followers.

2.   **Create Great Content:** Use your marketing time to concentrate on getting good content for your Tweets. Although it might seem easy to link in headlines or articles related to the business, you might do better by voicing an opinion about the article, providing a link at the bottom.

3.   **Follow Interesting People:** If you have found a person that you are interested in, either as someone in your line of business, or just someone who you can admire, follow them. These people are another way of adding value to your Twitter feed. While you might collect a lot of fans who won't create any interest among followers, a celebrity or famous brand might work well for you.

4.   **Follow your Rivals:** It might seem like a strange idea, but following your rivals can be very helpful. Firstly, people who like the industry's products are more likely to be interested in your business, and secondly, your followers like to feel like they have a choice. Connecting to your rival also implies friendly relations, something that Twitter etiquette encourages.

5.   **Use the Right Form and Style:** Twitter style is helpful in putting together certain types of Tweets, such as replies, retweets and acknowledgements. Using good form and style makes people feel confident in your Twitter feed, and will also ensure that they have a good opinion of your brand.

Whenever you are on Twitter, always remember the basic rules of politeness and good social manners. Don't say anything you wouldn't want your family to hear, and be gentle with your followers. While rule-breakers might attract attention for a while, most followers will quickly leave when they realize you just don't know how to be polite on a social networking site.

Keeping Twitter Etiquette Means Not Using Bots or Follower Tricks

Gathering followers on Twitter can be difficult and time-consuming. For businesses who want to promote a brand, or sell a new product, this can be very frustrating, and it might seem as though followers are never going to appear. Trending on Twitter will always take a long time when you are starting from scratch, and so many turn, in desperation, to companies who promise to boost follower accounts for a small payment. It might seem too good to be true - and that is exactly what it is, because companies who use this method could be putting their reputations at risk.

Another area where most businesses feel that they are not succeeding is in the creation and delivery of Tweets. Tweeting is, of course, what being part of Twitter is all about, but creating the perfect feed can be difficult. Even more difficult is generating this content day in, day out. Busy company owners, who may not have the time to create a new Twitter post each day, may decide instead to use robots to 'fill in' the 140 characters with information which is relevant to the business, or to the follower clicking on the link. However, just like with the paid followers, using robots to create Tweets is bad for the long-term reputation of the business.

Using Robots and Follower Tricks

The market for these Twitter fakes has never been stronger. There are dozens of businesses dedicated to selling Robot programs or fake followers, and the number is rising. This is despite the fact that there are now products designed to help Twitter users determine which is real and which is fake. Estimates currently suggest that there are more than 20 million fake accounts, dedicated to creating followers for a paying customer, and earning the account holder more than $40 million each year. These fake followers are purchased as a job lot, with a thousand at a time being sold for less than $20, and it is common for buyers to purchase dozens of these job lots each time. There were even rumors during the presidential campaign that one of the candidates bought 100,000 followers, increasing his fan base overnight. Whether that was true or not, the fact is that many businesses are turning to these fake accounts to increase the number of followers on their Twitter feed. These fake followers offer their buyers the chance to look more creditable, and more established than they really are. However, buying these followers is not always a good idea. The biggest problem for users of fake followers is that they are easy to spot, and real Twitter users are likely to be scornful of anyone who buys in their fan club.

Twitter Bots fall into a similar category of a seemingly beneficial application which is likely to lose real followers and create a bad name for the business. These programs are designed to reduce the amount of work that a business Twitter user has to do on their own. These computer programs are used to simulate your response to a particular comment by another user, or to create auto-posts containing promotions. Automation can be the key to getting better performance from your Twitter feed, but it can also be a bad idea if you want to retain your credibility and keep genuine followers. Perhaps the biggest downside to these robots is that they cannot create dynamic content - Tweets generated by interaction with followers. With the trend in Twitter moving towards 'conversation' as the preferred communication method, robots that are unable to respond sensibly to comments are becoming obvious and even ridiculous. The Bank of America's robot fail is one example of how robots have a negative impact in the long term.

Fake Followers and Twitter Etiquette

The temptation to buy fake followers can be rapidly reduced when users realize that they could face suspension or even exile from Twitter for using this method to increase their ratings. But there are even consequences for those who are not penalized by Twitter. These consequences are primarily to do with how your followers view you, and your brand.

The rankings on Twitter are designed to allow people to view feeds which are interesting or topical. Lifting yourself up through the ranks using fake followers is giving real-life viewers a fake impression of your popularity. It means that you are betraying one of the principles of Twitter - that it is a site for human interaction and socializing. Companies who keep to this principle should be rewarded for effort, so essentially anyone buying false followers is cheating.

Automation and Twitter Etiquette

It is possible to automate almost all of your Twitter posts using your account settings. These software programs allow you to take feeds from your website, or automate replies to new followers, or making it possible to add mentions of more than one user at once. All of these are allowed (with modifications in some cases) by Twitter. What is not allowed is the practice of automating a reply to a popular Twitter feed (called 'trending topics'), particularly when that involves unrelated topics. However, a big problem caused by automated programs which can be purchased from independent sellers is the repetitive Tweet. This is a single comment, usually a promotion or advertisement, which is sent to the Twitter feed at specified intervals. This is generally not accepted.

Using automated programs like this is frowned upon by

many in the social media industry. Firstly, it breaks the rules of Twitter etiquette which require that a user fully interact with their followers, and refrains from spamming them with worthless sales copy. Secondly, it is seen as quite rude to respond to every conversation with the same 'Hi there!' automated reply. Twitter users don't come to your feed to interact with a robot. They want to exchange ideas and information with a real person. Dropping the automated programs can make a significant difference to your follower numbers.

Keeping Twitter Etiquette

The rules of Twitter etiquette are generally unwritten, but one thing which all users agree on is that the use of any automated processes, from followers to thank-you messages, is not acceptable. Most businesses have joined Twitter in order to better connect with their fans and followers, and so using automated responses would clearly defeat the main purpose of their Twitter feed. It will also betray the followers who have joined because they are genuinely interested in the business - all they get will be false rankings and a robotic reply. This can have a negative impact on the brand, as followers associate it with cheating and lack of manners.

Keeping to Twitter Etiquette means completing Tweets and climbing the rankings by your own efforts. While it may seem like much harder work, requiring a lot more focus and commitment, the end result will be much better for the business, and for your relationship with the general public. Using fake followers is, for many Twitter users, the end of any chance for a real connection between themselves and the business. So ensuring that you have that communication by encouraging your own followers can be the best way to climb the rankings.

Keeping to Twitter etiquette also has its own advantages. Firstly, that etiquette is aimed at creating genuine links between businesses and customers, something that can only benefit the business. Secondly, good manners and politeness are more easily managed through direct communication. Without automation you are less likely to spam your followers, and more likely to create better content. Good relationships with your fans and good content are both key to rising up the ranks and staying there. It is not possible to do this using automated followers or messages.

As Twitter managers clamp down on the use of follower bots and automation, so keeping within the rules of Twitter etiquette can also help you to escape the negative consequences of using automated processes. Some businesses have been banned from the social networking site after using fake followers, and Twitter has even banned their IP address, meaning they won't be able to create another account. Businesses have also been in trouble for using automated messages, particularly ones which hijack unrelated topics. It is possible to be banned for that, whether it is deliberate or accidental due to your use of automation.

Keeping within the bounds of Twitter etiquette means not using bots or tricks to increase your follower numbers. However, it does mean creating your own, genuine followers, and improving your brand's reputation for honesty and commitment. Those are positive virtues which can be associated with products and with the business in general, and you are likely to get more followers from these actions than you could expect from choosing software programs. In addition, the connections you will make will be more authentic, and therefore longer-lasting, ensuring that your brand carries its positive reputation for a long time. By rejecting the use of bots and bought followers, Twitter users can expect to benefit through good content and good communication with real followers.

Overuse of Hashtags Breaks the Rules of Twitter Etiquette

The Hashtag has become one of the most influential communication styles to emerge from Twitter. Originally developed in order to ensure that users can find conversations relating to a single theme, or to a specific subject, they have now spread too many other aspects of social life. The use of Hashtags only began in 2007, surprisingly since they seem to have been around forever, when one Twitter user invited followers to vote on how they felt about using a sign (the Hashtag #) to co-ordinate conversations. This idea was quickly accepted and, within only a few months, users all over Twitter were adding this symbol to Tweets in order to emphasize their points. Most often, the Tweet contains a simple sentence, followed by the Hashtag and then a word, such as #etiquette, for example. This use means that followers can understand the purpose behind a Tweet that much more easily.

There is a downside to Hashtags, however, and that is when they are used excessively, incorrectly, or in a manner which is likely to confuse people. Studies suggest that followers are likely to be turned off by the constant use of Hashtags in a Tweet, or in a conversation. They can also be very intrusive when used to promote business or commercial interests at the end of an unrelated Tweet. Sometimes businesses have also alienated their followers by popping up in general conversation, complete with Hashtags relating to their products. In most cases, this is simply a matter of over-enthusiasm which is uncomfortable for other viewers, but in other cases, it can be a matter of poor business strategy which focuses upon selling rather than relationship building.

The simple fact is that Twitter etiquette rules are particularly strict when it comes to the overuse or misapplication of Hashtags. Although these rules are unofficial, for the most part there is a consensus about the use of Hashtags, and where they should be placed. Failure to observe these rules can lead to the account holder being shunned or ignored, and will certainly create a negative image of the business. While sticking to the rules of Hashtag Twitter etiquette cannot guarantee that you will be able to get a good response to your Tweets, it can certainly help your reputation, and the reputation of your brand. By following the rules, you can make use of them to enhance your communications, and select only the best Hashtags to retweet in order to collect more followers.

Hashtag Rules

Perhaps the most important aspect to any use of Hashtags is making sure that you limit their use. Although it can seem counter-intuitive to moderate your use of these fashionable and popular symbols, all too often the over-use of Hashtags makes any communication completely meaningless, both to your followers, and to anyone else who might be interested. Too many in one communication will overwhelm the reader, and may mean that they decide to stop following you.

The Hashtag rules are simple and easy to follow:

- **Don't Use Too Many Words:** If you place a Hashtag at the end of every word in a Tweet, or in a sentence, then people will find it hard to follow what you are saying. The basic principle of Tweeting is that it allows you to convey a simple, clear message, and the overuse of Hashtags can easily result in confusion. When it comes to a choice between a simple, clear post, and one heavily dosed with

Hashtags, it is not hard to work out which one the average user would prefer.

• **Don't Use Too Many Words in one Hashtag:** Some Tweeters have tried to get around the average readers dislike of too many Hashtags in one post by using one tag, and writing the words together, like this: #seeallofmyotherposts. This is hard to read, and while it is a good idea to put two words together under the same Tweet in order to make your message clear, writing out a sentence in this way is neither effective, nor easy on the eyes. The problem can be partially solved by adding a capital at the start of each word, but the best solution of all is to limit the amount of words you put together.

• **Don't Use Hashtags with the Same Word:** Another common problem for Tweet readers is the reoccurring tag. This is when a Twitter user adds more than one word, with the same general meaning, to the end of a post, such as #Promotion #ProductPlacement #MarketingPloy. While using your Hashtag for these phrases can ensure that your blog post or website gets more backlinks (because each # means that the words following are a hyperlink), but it can overcrowd your posts and make them difficult for people to read.

• **Don't Use Popular Hashtags Unless They Are Relevant:** Marketing Twitter users can sometimes make the mistake of including a popular Hashtag in their Tweet without having a real connection to the meaning. Although you might want to promote your new product to the general public, doing so by using a Tweet which is unconnected to your business makes no sense. You are not going to bring in more potential customers for your product through the use of Hashtags about the latest celebrity gossip, but you might alienate genuine followers, and earn yourself a reputation as a bandwagon-follower, which will do your business no good at all.

How to Get the Best from Hashtag Use

While there are many easy mistakes to make when using Twitter, they are also very useful tools when it comes to making sure that you get your message across on the micro-messaging format. Hashtags are also so popular that communicating without them could leave you isolated from popular trends. Readers might not be so keen to join with you if you cannot use Hashtags correctly, so it makes sense to learn how to use them effectively right from the start.

Firstly, you need to stick to the principles of Tweeting, which is communicating in a neat, precise way. This means restricting yourself to Hashtags which are relevant, and which can be seen to be relating to your subject. If necessary, you can easily explain what your tags mean in an individual Tweet, giving your readers the lowdown on your shorthand. No matter how badly you want to use the tags which are 'trending', if they are not connected to your Tweet, they will irritate your followers, and also annoy those who are using the popular Hashtag correctly. Whenever you use a Hashtag, aim for clarity.

Clarity in fact should be one of the aims of a Hashtag, since when used correctly they can help to illuminate a Tweet, or point readers to a blog post where you expand on the Tweet, or a related discussion on Twitter or Facebook. This clarity should also be remembered when you are using Hashtags which relate to previous discussions among your followers. It is common for Twitter users to take names, and created shorthand versions of them to use as Hashtags, but that does not mean that all of your followers will understand.

Focus your attention upon creating tags which are easy to follow, understand and re-use. This will help to organize your content and show where your comments have been retweeted.

Another important element in creating useful Hashtags is to ensure that they have value. Twitter is all about creating content which adds value to the discussion, or to your followers, and the Hashtags should be no exception. If you are using a Hashtag and is doesn't actually add anything to the content above it, leave it out. Only use them when they serve a constructive purpose. Overusing 'empty' Hashtags breaks all the rules of Twitter Etiquette, and will drive followers away.

If you have selected a useful, clear Hashtag, then you can do a lot with it. One Hashtag which relates to your business can also be used to link to other companies in the same industry, using the Hashtag on your own posts to create interest. You could also add the Hashtag during corporate events, and encourage people to use it in their own posts. This extends the influence of the Hashtag. Finding the right Hashtag for this purpose is essential, so it is a good idea to hold off on adding them until you have a good idea of what your audience wants.

When you have developed your Hashtag using the advice above, you can then go one step further, and start to track them online using tools designed to follow conversations and spot the # which relates to your business. Following your Hashtags as they spread through your followers can give you a great sense of achievement, and they also allow you to take note of which tags were successful, and which have not been taken up. This data will allow you to streamline your Tweets turning them into something which will enhance the reputation of your brand.

<u>Monetizing Twitter</u>

<u>Creating a Target Audience</u>

Much of the success of Twitter marketing begins at the most basic level, which involves developing and encouraging a target audience. The target audience that you need will hear exactly what you're saying, look for the products and services that you are offering, and then help you to build your audience even more with retweets and sharing information. Needless to say, it is very important that you develop a target audience that will look forward to your Tweets.

Why should you even consider marketing on Twitter anyway? Twitter is becoming more and more popular, and it is more social than any of the other social media platforms that are available today. On a day to day basis, people are retweeting what other people are saying, they're sharing links with one another, and doing a variety of other things that encourage interaction and sharing ideas. To date, there are over 200 million users that utilize Twitter on a regular basis for a variety of reasons.

Due to the increased popularity, marketing on Twitter just makes sense. But it's not a simple as it may be on a website like Facebook or Google Plus. It actually involves a lot more effort on your part when it comes to building your audience and spreading your message. On Facebook, you just need to nab followers and then get your message out there. On Twitter, you have to interact with those who follow you in order to keep their attention and their interest.

So what can you do in order to create a target audience? How can you start to get people following your Tweets and spreading the word about your market and message? Here are some tips that can help you to get a Twitter following and expand it into an audience that pays.

1. **Start with a Plan.** The time you will spend thinking through what you want to accomplish using Twitter will pay big dividends; particularly because most Twitter users don't have a plan. The fact that you have taken the time to work one out will give you a big advantage. Start with defining what brand you are interested in establishing and expanding. Then focus on the characteristics of your ideal 'follower' and those you intend to follow. With these set, you can begin to build a network that will help you advance your interests.

2. **Developing content even before you have an audience.** It sounds incredibly simple, but it can really make a huge difference when you're trying to develop a target audience. What sorts of things would you want your target audience to be interested in? Do you have insider information or other information that could be relevant to potential followers? Make sure that you're keeping up to date with current news and

the topics that are trending on Twitter and utilize them into your Twitter feed. Some social media experts will recommend that you put as much as one to two weeks of content up before you start becoming assertive with trying to develop a following. Some people may start following you organically as well, so make sure you welcome and utilize those followers as soon as they show up.

3.   **Share your Twitter feed with those closest to you.** Your friends, loved ones, and colleagues are an instant network that you can tap into. Tell them about your Twitter feed and share with them your goals and purposes behind it. Many times, these people will be incredibly supportive and can help you to expand your network by talking with their friends and loved ones. We've all got a natural, supportive network available to tap into; don't feel guilty when you decide to pursue it and use it. Most likely, they will be willing and even eager to help you get followers and other resources.

4.   **Subscribe to relevant Twitter feeds.** After you've got some content on the site, it's time for you to start being assertive about going after people that you want in your audience. A good way to start doing this is by subscribing to Twitter feeds that talk about topics which are related to yours. For example, if your company is one that sells farming products, you will want to follow Twitter feeds relating to agriculture, farming, and other related topics.

The Twitter feeds that you follow can help feed information into your own feed and you can retweet some of what they're saying in order to create awareness. Many times, the feeds that you follow will follow you back as well. When they do that, they will likely do the same thing for you without you even asking; that's why you need to continue to post relevant and interesting information on a consistent basis. If you peter off, even just a little, people may start to lose interest and forget that you're there.

5.   **Follow those that you want to follow you.** This is a very assertive tactic, but it works. Twitter eliminates geography and makes it so that people who think similarly can connect with one another online. That means that you have more opportunities than you ever have before to connect with people, even those who are in niche markets. That means that your audience is likely already out there, you just have to go find them.

How do you do this? There are a couple ways to go about it. First, you can search for users in a variety of ways. Twitter's user search uses the information that people have given them and returns search results. For example, if you run a business that involves video games and gaming, then you can search for users who like those things as well. If you run a business in a particular region, you can search for users that are in your area that may be interested in what you are doing. If your business has online services, then you will be able to reach an even wider audience. When you find the users that you'd like to follow, follow them and invite them to follow your feed as well!

6.   **Dive into the conversation.** You will see all types of conversations as you journey through the Twitterverse. Some of them are just for entertainment, but some of them will be incredibly relevant to the products and services that you are providing. Get involved in conversations and interject your own thoughts. Getting into conversations on Twitter can

help with several aspects of the audience building process.

- • It helps to establish your expertise and allows you to share your knowledge.
- • It helps to expand your influence to those who follow the person(s) that you are having conversations with, even if they are not following you at the time of the conversation.
- • It helps to get the word out about you and what you are doing.
- • If the conversation is with individuals that follow you, it helps to give your company and your Twitter feed a "face."

Conversations can be an enjoyable experience as well, especially if you like to share the knowledge that you have. Be respectful, be willing to learn, and provide relevant and interesting information to those who are involved and watching the conversation(s). Don't be shy; the more of a voice that you have, the more influence you will have and the larger audience you will gain.

7. **Try Live Tweeting.** Live tweeting is a relatively new phenomenon, but you can see why it would be useful for those who are looking to broaden their audience and keep them engaged. If your followers are interested in the industry you are in and you go to a conference or talk, go ahead and live tweet. Live tweeting can be a lot of fun and is very organic. Be tactful, but share your thoughts and provide information that you learn as you are learning it. Your followers will really enjoy it, and it can be a great way to get more followers as they retweet the things that you are sharing through live tweeting.

8.   **Be Relevant.** I've alluded to this in almost every section of this article, but this is something that you need to keep in mind no matter what method you are trying in order to develop your audience. It's also important for you to remember during the entire time that you are working on your Twitter feed. What can you do in order to stay relevant? Here are some suggestions.

- Keep up with news events, both those that are relevant to your industry and are relevant to almost anyone. Link articles, make mention of certain events, and get into conversations about relevant news topics.
- Always make sure to share new and relevant information about the industry that you are working in. You don't have to be on top of breaking news, but being abreast of that information can keep your followers interested.
- Keep your followers in the loop. If there are changes coming to your company, promotions that you are running, or new services or products that you are offering, let them know on Twitter.
- Be friendly and approachable. It's perfectly acceptable to ask your followers how they're doing or what they've been up to. It's also acceptable to share an amusing message or photo that you think will be appealing to your audience.
- Retweet, retweet, and retweet some more. It gives you more credibility and shows that you're up to date on what's going on in the Twitter-verse.

I hope that these tips will help you as you advance on your journey with Twitter and creating your target audience. The sooner that you develop an engaged, interested audience, the easier it will be for you to market your goods, services, or other information to more and more people. Twitter marketing can be incredibly challenging due to the immense amount of interactivity involved, but it can also be very rewarding.

<u>Monetizing Twitter by Utilizing Keywords</u>

Social media has become more popular over the past decade, and has become the primary source of news and information for many people around the world. We've gone from consuming media in the form of newspapers and magazines to a more interactive model, where we both create and consume. This can be a very good thing, because it allows the consumer to have more of a voice than they ever had before. But it can cause a lot of problems for those who run businesses.

Those who run businesses are likely to be used to the model of consumption; they produce advertisements on TV, in the newspaper, or in a magazine, and people respond to seeing those advertisements. Can that still be utilized? Absolutely, but with the internet, you have to be a little more creative with it. You need to assertively target your audience and make sure that that audience is getting the information that you want it to get about your company and the goods and services that it offers.

There are a variety of ways you can do that, but social media (specifically, Twitter) is the best way for you to reach out to potential customers and get that information into their hands. One of the ways that you can help reel people in is to make sure that you are utilizing keywords (in the form of the famous "hashtag (#)") in such a way that they benefit you.

What is a Keyword?

A keyword is a word, phrase, or even a question that people use in a search engine to find particular information about a certain topic. Say that I wanted to find somewhere to stay on a visit to Virginia Beach, VA. I may search for "hotels in

Virginia Beach." At that point, a variety of results will come up, and most of them are webpages for particular hotels in Virginia Beach. Other pages that may come up are travel guides or other resources. As long as the phrase "hotels in Virginia Beach" is located somewhere within the webpage, it will come up as a result somewhere.

Many times, businesses will use search engine optimization methods in order to drive traffic to their site. This involves many different factors, and many of them depend on the use of keywords. The higher up your website is on search results, the more likely it is that someone will come upon your site. It's estimated that 70% of the time, people will click on a search result on the first page of results.

So, why does this matter to you if you are using social media? Keywords do matter, because Twitter has a search engine that you can use to find tweets about certain topics. Many times, they use the hashtag (#) even though you can find search results that don't utilize the hashtag feature as well.

Why Am I Using a Hashtag to Signify Keywords?

In the Twitter-verse (a slang term for the world of Twitter) keywords are often signified by using what are called "hashtags." Where did these come from and why are these used?

Actually, it was suggested by someone outside of Twitter's Chris Messina mentioned on his blog that Twitter needed to do something in order to tag posts of interest in a specific field, or to signify keywords. Here's what he said in that 2007 post:

"Every time someone uses a channel tag to mark a status,

not only do we know something specific about that status, but others can eavesdrop on the context of it and then join in the channel and contribute as well. Rather than trying to ping-pong discussion between one or more individuals with daisy-chained @replies, using a simple #reply means that people not in the @reply queue will be able to follow along, as people do with Flickr or Delicious tags."

Nate Ritter, a resident of San Diego, used the first hashtags after that to talk about the San Diego Fire (#sandiegofire) just days after Messina mentioned using them. In July of 2009, Twitter officially "adopted" the hash tag and began to hyperlink all hashtags in tweets to Twitter search results for the hashtagged word (and commonly misspelled words and their respective spellings). In 2010, Twitter introduced "Trending Topics" on the Twitter front page. Trending topics is there for the purpose of displaying hashtags that are rapidly becoming popular on the site, which will usually give you an idea of what the "hot topics" are around the world that day.

So Why Does This All Matter for Me?

Alright, so why does this matter? Why should you care about the history and development of hashtags and what keywords are? Because hashtags and keywords are two very important pieces of the puzzle that you will be putting together when you wade into using social media for monetization and marketing.

Here's a great analogy about social media. Many people look at media and consider it to be an electrical wire. The generators create the electricity, feed it through the wire, and it is consumed by products that use electricity. Before social media, this was a good analogy. The generator of media was the news outlets; the wire was newspapers and magazines, and the electricity-using products are those who read them. Many people assume that the internet works the same, and in some cases, it does. You use a search engine, get the information you need, and move on.

The analogy breaks down when social media comes into the picture. Social media suddenly brings in tons and tons of content creators, so that means there are literally millions of generators all trying to get to the same people. You can't think in the same restricted ways, so you have to find a way to sift through the mess and get information out to people.

That's where the hashtag comes in; it's a versatile way to separate information into categories that people can look for. And, instead of the old conventional way of forcing people to pick a category, you can create hashtags as you see fit and necessary. The solution to the problem of messy, disorganized information is allowing the people who are creating the content to develop their own structure to it as they build it. The hashtag solves that problem, and also creates answers for you to use in your marketing and monetization.

How Can I Make Hashtags Work for Me?

This is what you've been waiting for. Hashtags can help you with a variety of different things. Here are some of the benefits of using hashtags.

- You can use them to get involved in conversations about products, services, and/or other topics related to your company

- If you use hashtags from the "Trending Topics" on Twitter's homepage, you can increase your exposure and gain more regular followers
- Hashtags can help you to target particular people who would benefit from following you
- You can coin your own hashtag keywords and use them to brand your business

These aren't the only reasons that it is beneficial either; get creative with your hashtags and keyword usage and you will start to see a lot more people following you.

Tips for using Hashtags

So you still aren't used to using hashtags? Here are six tips that can help you use hashtags effectively and without irritating your followers.

1.   If you brand your company with its own hashtag, those who like what you're doing can use the hashtag and point back to your company or product. For example, Amazon frequently uses #goldbox and #KindleFire; Home Depot uses #HDHacks when they give home design tips. This will help make your Twitter look innovative and it will help people to be able to identify your company as the source. As a result, they may start following you!

2.   Do not overdo the hashtags! Twitter has a 140 character limit; don't load half of those characters with hashtag fodder. Write out something useful or informative and tag on one to three hashtags in the tweet. Use them naturally.

3.   Don't use "all caps" in your hashtags. Both of those indicate to potential followers that you are probably trying way too hard to use hashtags and seem almost "desperate" in your marketing. #CHECKITOUT looks unprofessional; #checkitout is much more relaxed.

4.   Don't use more than two or three words in your hashtags. Hashtags that look like #Checkoutourhugeannualsale are obnoxious and just ate up most of your tweet. Stick to #annualsale. On that same vein, if your company has several words in its name, come up with some sort of abbreviation to make it shorter. For example, if your company is named Jim and Bob's Farmer's Market, go ahead and use #JBFarmMarket or even #JimandBob as a hashtag. Doesn't that look much cleaner than #JimandBobsFarmMarket? Exactly.

5.   Don't be too broad with your keywords. Going with our Jim and Bob's Farmers Market example, if you were just to use #farmermarket or #farmmarket, it could really get lost in everything. Those bland hashtags are fine if you are a general user that isn't trying to get followers, but if you're using Twitter for monetization, it's going to fall on its face. Use hashtags that may fall into categories of keywords where your posts are some of the only ones that show up. That way, you can grab onto your target audience better.

6.   This tip is more for companies that have a brick-and-mortar location or provide services within a particular geographic region. Do not be afraid of using #NYC or #Philly (or whatever city, town, county, or region you live in). That will help target people within

your particular geographic reason and cause more people to look your way.

Now that we've taken a deeper look into hashtags and how they work, how do you feel about the process? Do you think it's something that you can do without a lot of issues? Knowing is half the battle, and even though there are literally thousands of tips that we could provide to you for Twitter marketing, a lot of it is testing and trying things. If something you try doesn't work, try something else.

Product Promotion and Affiliate Links on Twitter

Are you looking to make your Twitter more effective for monetization? One of the best ways to get money on Twitter is to promote other companies and other people's products and services. You can do this in two major ways: Product promotion and affiliate marketing. If you own a business, have written a book, or affiliate with a company like Amazon, you can use focused links and create yourself some revenue by using these two methods. Let's take a look at both of these methods and see how you can use them for your benefit.

What is Product Promotion?

Sometimes, you can get a company, an author, or whatever else to pay you some extra revenue by promoting their business, brand, or a particular product on Twitter by using hashtags and/or. An example of this is Bob Harper (from the Biggest Loser) and his promotion of Quaker oats and oatmeal. Once every few days, you will see an advertisement on Bob's page that includes @Quaker and #ad or #quakeroats. He is getting money from Quaker for promoting their product.

Getting involved in product promotion is fairly simple. Many companies will be involved with several platforms that help connect them to interested parties that want to promote their products (TwittAd is one of the most popular). If you have a personal connection to a small business or an author, you may be able to connect with them and get paid per tweet as well. Getting involved with product promotion depends a lot on your own connections and how much effort you want to put into it.

Promoted Tweets are actually encouraged by Twitter. Promoted tweets are regular, everyday tweets that purchased by advertisers that want to reach out to potential customers and get people talking about their product. They are always labeled as "Promoted" and can be retweeted like any other tweet. If you want to learn more, check out Twitter's support page on <u>Promoted Tweets</u>.

What is Affiliate Marketing?

Affiliate marketing allows those who are advertising products on their Twitter or their blog to get a portion of the sales generated by their advertising. The reason that companies do this is because those who produce those items can get a lot of advertising for a lower cost than they would by buying ads. The person who is marketing is at an advantage too; if they do their job correctly and well, the marketer can get a nice chunk of change out of it as well.

Affiliate marketing is offered through a variety of different programs, and many of them are fairly easy to join. For the most point, try to avoid the affiliate programs that require you to pay (there are some that are legitimate, but most of the best ones have free sign-up and free membership. Before you join any affiliate marketing program, do research and see how much other people like using them. We have a few suggestions here for you to check out as well.

Some Affiliate Programs That You Can Try Out

There are a variety of affiliate programs out there that you can try. Here are some of the most popular ones that people are using in the Twitter-verse.

- **Tweet Adder Affiliate Program.** This program is for the marketing and management software known as Tweet Adder. You can get as much as 50% commission for each direct sale referral. They have a tiered system of affiliates that you can check out as well.

- **Groupon Partner Network.** Do you like saving tons of money on Groupon? So do a lot of other people. Their program, also known as GPN, can help you to keep saving money and also start earning money as well.

- **LivingSocial Affiliate Program.** Just like Groupon, LivingSocial allows you to post affiliate links and earn some cash as you share their great deals.

- **ChaCha Affiliate Program.** This program is great if you like to share funny stories or random information. You can share their tweets and make some cash. Want more info? Check out their affiliate FAQ page.

- **Amazon Associates.** Amazon has some pretty cool affiliate perks, and you can get up to 10% with certain affiliations. Their Amazon Associates program has more information, but their program is awesome because Amazon literally has thousands of products available for affiliate marketing.

- **Ad.ly.** Ad.ly is an affiliate program designed especially for Twitter (the others above are for any blog or social media). They have a variety of opportunities available.

- **SponsoredTweets.com**. You would actually be sending promotional tweets with SponsoredTweets, and you would set your price per tweet, set the dollar amount, and some keywords related to the things that you normally post on Twitter. Then, you wait for some offers to come in and you tweet those tweets.

Tips for Promoting Products and Doing Affiliate Marketing

Now that you know some of the places that you can go (and you've probably signed up for some of them if you're truly interested), what can you do to tweet those promotions and affiliate links effectively? These are some general tips that will be able to help you whether you are trying to promote products for someone or if you are working as an affiliate marketer.

Don't post anything that doesn't interest you or your audience.

Some people wrongly assume that the more affiliate and promotional posts you do, the better. This isn't true; stick to what you know. Say that most of what you tweet about has to do with gaming and video games. You aren't going to post links that talk about makeup or jewelry, because the people that follow you on Twitter will likely get very annoyed and may stop following you. Post affiliate and promotional tweets that are related to things that your audience would be interested in.

Don't post anything you wouldn't truly recommend.

Why would you waste your time promoting something that you actually don't care about? You want to promote products that you've actually tried or products from a company that you get other products for. Going with the gaming example from the previous point, you don't want to promote a video card from a company that you don't normally buy your gaming computer parts from. Stick with what you know or products that your friends or colleagues have used and liked.

You don't have to stick with the "conventional" ways of posting links.

Don't feel like you only have to pop an affiliate or promoted tweet up and call it a day. You can use those same links in conversations or in response to the Trending Topics of the day if they are relevant. Utilize your hashtags to the best of your ability, and just get creative with the process. The more creative you are, the more organic it will feel and the more likely it will be for you to get the clicks and purchases that you need in order for your efforts to be worthwhile.

Make your posts unique.

Unless the affiliate or promotional company asks you to do a specific tweet, you don't have to stick to the script. Be creative, use your own voice, and make your posts stand out. The less fabricated that your promotional posts sound, the most honest and sincere they will be appear to be to your audience. That will increase the likelihood of your audience actually checking out the links and maybe even buying the products you're mentioning. If they feel you are being insincere in your tweets, they may perceive you as being a "sell-out" and just ignore those posts.

Don't overload your audience.

This is, perhaps, the most important tip that we have for you. Do not overload your audience with promotional tweets. If your audience wanted to get slammed with advertisements, they would watch TV or watch YouTube. If you overload them, they'll start to feel like your Twitter feed is just about advertisements. Be picky about when and how often that you're putting up affiliate and promotional links, and you will see a lot more success than you would if you spammed them.

One Last Thought: Using Both Twitter and a Blog Together For Maximum Effectiveness

Many people who monetize their Twitters will make this suggestion. Why? Because if you use your Twitter alone, it could start to look unprofessional and people may get sick of your affiliate links. A much more subtle approach is to link your blog posts that mention the affiliate links in them or have relevant affiliate links in the sidebar. If you go with this approach, it's going to take a lot more time and energy. Many people who have Twitters are already bloggers as well, so that lends itself to this tip. If you haven't started blogging yet, maybe you could consider starting? It's worth a try at the very least, and if it doesn't work, then you can drop the blog and go back to strictly Twitter.

If you decide to go with this approach, make sure that you follow some of the same tips that you're reading here. Don't overload your audience, make sure that the affiliate and promotional links feel organic, and only post relevant links. If you don't follow these, the blog will just seem like a cheap way for you to get more characters. Make sure that the blog is a legitimate blog, with posts that don't include affiliate links, and then it will feel like you're actually giving genuine suggestions instead of just trying to make money.

As you can see, there are a variety of things that you have to take into account in order to effectively monetize your Twitter using product promotion and affiliate links. If you keep all of this in mind as you get started, you will be more likely to be successful in your endeavors. It may take a while to get the proper audience and get people who will purchase the products that you are sharing, but if you hold out for the long run and keep hustling, you will see results.

Tools that Will Make Your Twitter Feed Shine

Are you still getting started with your Twitter? The process of monetizing your Twitter starts with regular Tweeting, planning, and organizing. There are a ton of tools out there that you can utilize in order to make this process easier. In this article, we're going to take a look at a few of the most popular ones and give you some ideas as to which ones to consider.

Get People to Spread the Word for Freebies

CloudFlood is one of the best tools out there for giving away freebies on your website, if you use your website in conjunction with a Twitter feed. This tool allows you to offer an electronic product in exchange for Tweets. This is so that you can get more exposure; contests and freebies will always people to do help you out with your marketing. It's a fairly simple process. You create an electronic product; it can be an eBook, it can be a eGift Card, it can be a percent off of services, or it can be anything that you want to offer to your fans. Then, you create a link to that product and go to CloudFlood's site to create a link. Fill out the information on their easy-to-use form:

- The Name of Your Freebie.
- The Link to Your Freebie.
- What you want people to Tweet when they click the share button.
- The link to your blog, or any site you want to promote.

136

That's it! It's a piece of cake. Put in the Captcha code, create the button. Copy the HTML code, put it near the image for your free item, and watch as people redeem their freebies and you get more traffic to your site and more followers on your Twitter.

Allow multiple contributors with GroupTweet

GroupTweet is a pretty neat Twitter tool if there are several people who contribute to a Twitter feed. This app essentially makes it really easy for many people (there is no upper limit) to Tweet from the same account. GroupTweet is actually a very popular app for large organizations; universities have been using these for their public relations departments for a very long time.

What are some of the cool features that you get with Group Tweet? Here are some of the big ones:

- Content creation isn't solely dependent on one person. That means that your Twitter won't get dry by using the same sort of language all of the time, and more minds are working together to make innovative, creative content for your feed.

- Everyone has an individual password for the GroupTweet dashboard, so that they don't have to remember yet another password for another account.

- Those who have personal Twitter accounts can utilize GroupTweet from any Twitter client and device by using a hashtag (#) or a mention (@) to the GroupTweet account.

- Scheduling services are available so that you can post Tweets over a certain amount of time. This can help you to regulate all of the Tweets that are going through.

- The "owner" of the Twitter account associated with GroupTweet is able to moderate what the other posters are Tweeting on the account.

- You can utilize GroupTweet to consolidate and discuss topics within your GroupTweet group.

As you can see, GroupTweet is a great program for any group of people that are contributing content to one Twitter account without the person "in charge" of the account losing control over the content within. You can get really creative with GroupTweet's services and options, so definitely consider giving it a try if you can.

Give Twitter Followers Limited Access with OfferPop

OfferPop is a product that is similar to CloudFlood in the sense that you get to give your followers exclusive offers and content, but you don't necessarily have to have a website in order to utilize the program. Let's take a quick look at how you could use OfferPop to your advantage.

Say that you are selling an eBook. That eBook regularly costs $10 for people to purchase and download. That's great, but how are you going to get the word out? If you already have a Twitter feed, you can talk about it, but how are you actually going to get people to purchase it? That's where OfferPop sets in. You can offer retweet deals where, after a person retweets so many times, they can unlock a discount on your eBook. You can offer deals where if a

138

certain number of people retweet a status; your eBook will go on sale the next day. OfferPop makes it easy to track all of those logistics.

Here are some of the other ways that you can use OfferPop:

- By running open promotions or contests and including a unique hashtag
- Using game mechanics by setting customizable retweet counts to unlock deals
- Target deals and offers exclusively to followers
- Send discounts, promotions and other offers to new followers and participants in hashtag campaigns automatically through direct messaging
- Automatically generate landing pages for each campaign
- Build active fan bases
- Optimize social content
- Get full promocode and bar code support and in-depth campaign reporting

Marketers from all over the world use OfferPop for all of these reasons and more. OfferPop was actually the platform that was used to create and develop the first hashtag campaign that was featured during the Super Bowl, so you know that the platform is a big deal. Check out OfferPop today; even though it does have a regular cost, you can get a 14-day free trial so you can see how you like it before you buy.

TweetDeck

TweetDeck is a cool tool if you don't like the way that the Twitter interface looks. Essentially, it's a dashboard that works with the API of Twitter in order to give you more flexibility and insight when using Twitter as a marketing and/or monetization tool. Here are a few of the features that TweetDeck offers to its users.

- You can arrange your feeds in the way that you want to see them. They have the interface split into columns that you can use to organize your feeds in a way that makes sense to you.

- You can use Twitter as a desktop application instead of using it on your browser, which makes it more convenient. If you're like every other social media professional, you have too many tabs open on your browser as it is, so the desktop app is pretty cool.

- TweetDeck helps you to filter the information that you need in a more advanced way that you can using the standard Twitter API.

- If you have multiple accounts, TweetDeck may be a good option in terms of helping you organize and post from all of your Twitter accounts. In my opinion, that is not what TweetDeck is best utilized for; if you are just looking for a social media management system that covers multiple accounts, then I would suggest HootSuite, which is discussed more in the next section.

- TweetDeck has customizable alerts and notifications that you can develop in a way that best fits you and your purposes.

Whether or not you use TweetDeck is based on your preferences. Some people don't like the interface; other people think it's a huge improvement on what Twitter utilizes in its standard API. The only way for you to know is to check it out for yourself. Get an account with them and play around with it. The reason I mention it here is because it's the most popular Twitter dashboard and many people really enjoy using it.

Have Multiple Accounts? HootSuite is the Ticket

If you are working from multiple Twitter accounts or multiple social media accounts (Facebook, LinkedIn, Google+, etc), you absolutely must use a social media management system that helps you to post to multiple sites. If you do not, you will have a hard time keeping everything straight and figuring out exactly what you want to post and on which social media site. There are several of these platform-style websites out there, but the best one (which most social media professionals use) is HootSuite.

HootSuite allows you to manage all of those social media accounts and even lets you attach a variety of items to your Tweets, like pictures, videos, and documents. You can create schedules and even post the same Tweet to all of your accounts at the same time. You can even do some of the functions of the individual sites by using the HootSuite platform.

Another great thing about HootSuite is that it is Freemium; that is, if you have five or less social profiles to deal with, you can get it for free. If you decide that you want more social media profiles or features (they have some great ones for those who are big into analytics), then you can pay $5.99 a month to use their HootSuite Pro services. Trust me, you don't feel like you're missing anything if you use the free version; it's incredibly functional and easy to use. The premium tools are definitely for those who need take their

HootSuite and social media experience a step further.

I'll be honest: these are far from the only tools out there. There are literally thousands of Twitter tools and apps that help with contests, with scheduling Tweets, with keeping track of data, and with checking out logistics. Many of the Twitter tools that you can find online are worth the time and energy you put into them. Dozens of websites will give you lists of tools that you "should" and "shouldn't" be using, Find the ones with the interfaces that you like and the level of interaction and use that you need in order to increase your reach and market effectively.

Techniques to Avoid When Monetizing Social Media

When you're new to the social media scene, whether you are using it for marketing your business or for monetization, there are a lot of "tips and tricks" that will be thrown at you. And, being newer to the scene, you may try all of them. Why don't you try to take some time off of your efforts? Here are some techniques that you should completely avoid or forget about when trying to monetize or market using your Twitter.

Avoid "Rehearsed" Tweets

"Rehearsed" Tweets are absolutely dull, to be honest. Some people will schedule a random ad tweet during particular intervals in their tweeting. Sometimes it will be every five tweets, sometimes it will be every twenty, and in some cases it could be fifty or one-hundred tweets that go by before an ad comes up.

But the issue is, these tweets are incredibly rehearsed and they appear to be ingenuine. These "rehearsed Tweets" have a set makeup and sound the same every time they are posted. Usually, they're based on a script that you are given from the company you are advertising for. The problem with these rehearsed Tweets is that they totally ignore the interactivity and targeting that is a huge benefit for Twitter users who want to use their Tweets to make some extra cash.

Instead of copying and pasting rehearsed tweets, why don't you interact with your audience some more? Follow what they're saying, and post relevant Tweets that will give them information that is relevant to your interests and to the interests of your audience instead of signing up with companies that require you to follow a particular script.

Avoid Display Ads and Third Party Contexts

Display ads and third party contexts are fine if you are running a website or if you are on Facebook, but the problem with Twitter is that it's not really built for those types of advertising. Many people have seen a lot of success with ads from Google AdSense, but only if they have a regular website that they send people to check out. Display ads just don't have the same punch when you have to click on the link and then click on the advertisement.

You don't need to totally eliminate these from monetization, however. If you are like most people who are looking to earn money on the internet, you probably have a blog or website that you are using alongside of Twitter. If that's the case, then you can use these sorts of techniques on your website or blog. Most social media experts will tell you the same exact thing. Let the ads with pictures and video stay on your website; get creative with links and text on Twitter.

Avoid Anything That You Have to Pay For

If you have to pay in order to advertise for a company or to get cash per Tweet, it is most likely a scam, and should definitely be avoided. If a company or website is trying to make you pay, that is the money that they are using to stuff in their pockets and/or that is what they are using to pay other people who are doing the same things that you do. They are almost never legitimate and you will lose more money than you will actually make.

This piece of advice does not apply to apps or tools. If you are purchasing a license to use a tool that can help you with monetization (i.e. HootSuite Pro), that is completely fine, because that is how those companies make their money. You are paying for a product that is making your life more convenient, or for a license. Those companies are legitimate. This section is talking about those companies that tell you to pay a dollar amount so that you can learn how to make thousands of dollars a month; those are the scams that you have to worry about.

Avoid anything that is contrary to what you think, feel, or believe

If you look at a monetization opportunity and it makes you feel uncomfortable for any reason, then you should probably avoid it. Many people will sell their soul in order to try and make some money, but if the ads or the products you are being asked to promote are against the values that you hold, then it may be a good idea to avoid that monetization technique. It's not selfish or naïve; it's actually a question that many business owners will ask themselves as well.

Why is this important to talk about? Many times, people will feel sheepish or uncomfortable because they can make money with a company that uses crass humor, provides pornographic images, or promotes a lifestyle or belief system that they don't necessarily agree with. Money is never a reason for you to give up your values; if it makes you uncomfortable, would your audience be uncomfortable as well? Unless the answer to that question is definitely "no," you risk alienating and losing your audience as well. The possibility for earning money is not worth losing the Twitter audience that you've spent so much time building up.

Avoid oversaturating your market

Oversaturation will drive your audience crazy, no matter who is in your audience. If you are constantly inundating your audience with advertisement after advertisement, product promotion after product promotion, your audience is going to get bored. They're also going to become desensitized to it; eventually, your old monetization methods are going to not give you any money at all if you aren't careful.

Imagine if you saw the same advertisement every single day, several times a day. Or if, every time you went to a particular Twitter feed, it was spotted with advertisements and promotional products every other tweet. You'd probably stop following them, correct? Would you ever buy anything from them? Probably not, unless you saw something that was actually of interest to you. Then why would you try that method on your audience? Above, we talked about avoiding "rehearsed" Tweets; the same logic applies here. Allow your product promotion and your advertising to be more fluid and organic instead of forcing it into every nook and cranny where you assume it will fit.

Avoid providing Information instead of Conversation

Many companies go with the old model of advertising. Imagine that you are watching television; everything that you are doing is consumption, unless you are voting for American Idol or Survivor. You consume information, you consume advertisements, and you consume some junk as well. But you aren't providing anything to the conversation. The television is telling you all of these things. You may talk about them with other people, but you are not adding to the conversation. Much of advertisement and product promotion theory is based upon the assumption that media is consumed.

With the advent of the internet, this has totally changed. The internet and social media like Twitter in particular, are not places that you are given information and expected to consume it. The internet allows its users to interact with information and in places like Twitter; the consumers are also the content creators. That means you can't go with the old ways of advertising anymore.

That brings us to why this point (avoid providing information instead of conversation) is so important for anyone who is trying to monetize their social media. If you are just spitting out content, it's not necessarily going to do anyone any good. Instead, you need to drop hints in conversations, you need to allow people to share about the products you are promoting, and you need to make the process very organic. If you do not, then you are no different than a webpage that is full of spammy advertising, and no one is going to care about what you are saying.

Avoid Being Passive Instead of Assertive

Many people assume that, because it's the internet, then their social media will be found eventually. This is never a good technique to follow, especially if you are looking to turn a profit on your monetization efforts. You have to put some work into it; you will have to build your audience, you will have to make sure that you are getting the exposure that you need. You will have to be assertive; you can't just set up your Twitter and sit back.

How do you do this? Get involved in conversations, retweet posts that you like, and make your Twitter as engaging and interesting as possible. You have to earn the right to advertise and promote products on your Twitter; you do that by providing quality content and getting an audience that actually cares about what you are talking about. Assertiveness will get you much further than sitting back and expecting good things to come to you.

Obviously, this article telling you specific companies or websites that you should be avoiding. Instead, it's meant to be a guide that can help you discern whether or not a monetization program is worth your time and energy. There are a lot of scams out there that end up taking your money instead of giving you money, and so it's important to understand what may or may not be worth the effort. With time and effort (not get-rich-quick schemes), you will find that more legitimate techniques will help you make some extra cash. Good luck with your Twitter monetization efforts!

Why Your Business Should Use Promoted Accounts on Twitter

Businesses both large and small are choosing to turn to social media in order to reach more people and generate greater interest in their products. It has been estimated that around 200 million people belong to Twitter, and that reaching people through this medium is one of the best ways of spreading information about your brand, or about your business as a whole. Twitter is such a good source of marketing that businesses find themselves being drawn into the networking site. This means that there are more and more companies striving to get noticed, and hoping that their business will be the one that shoots to the top of the Twitter Rankings. In 2010, Twitter developed a Paid Advertisements system which was designed to help business owners manage social media more effectively. Rather than simply struggling on your own to make it, business owners can choose to use Twitter Promotions, including Promoted Tweets and Promoted Accounts, to generate more interest in their company.

Before making the decision to work with Promoted Accounts, it is a good idea to fully understand what it is, and what it can be used for. Twitter business users often want to reach people in order to generate interest in a new business product, brand, or connected companies. Promoted Accounts are there to help create an impact on Twitter, rather than on focused groups. They are designed to ensure that you can generate more interest in your Twitter page, and acquire more followers. In fact, Promoted Accounts appear on a page called 'Who to Follow', which began as rankings lists, indication who was most popular in particular fields. Promoted Accounts are therefore a more rapid way of singling out your business to people who would not otherwise have known that you were there. As an additional benefit, companies can choose to target specific groups of users, such as those who are likely to be interested in your particular products, or those who are popular and therefore might be able to expose your account to even more Twitter users. The use of Twitter Promoted Accounts can therefore not only help you to bring in more random followers, but also those who would have been keen to join your account in the first place.

Who to Follow

There are three main places where a Promoted Account will appear. By far the most important is known as the 'Who to Follow" widget, found on the Twitter homepage, or in Connect tabs. This widget is used to help users find other accounts that they might be interested in, and is a useful way to connect to people who might otherwise not have found you. Often, the accounts featured in Who to Follow are the most popular, or the most relevant, Twitter feeds, and so being able to place your own business among those accounts will add value to your Twitter page.

Other Locations

There are also other locations where Twitter displays Promoted Accounts. It is also possible to find your paid account promotion on 'Similar to you' promotions on profile pages, so more Twitter users will be exposed to your account, rather than just those on the Who to Follow page. In addition, users of Twitter will also find these Promoted Accounts when they search for people or subjects with a link to the business account. These accounts will appear on the Twitter user's suggestions box, as usual, although Promoted Accounts will show up with the mark "Promoted by (Business name)".

Reasons to Use Promoted Accounts

For a business, being able to use Promoted Accounts serves two purposes. Firstly, it encourages people to follow your Tweets, to see your comments about your company, and generally become more attached to the brand. Secondly, it displays your Twitter name (which should include your company name) to a much wider audience. Even if people looking at the Who to Follow page don't choose to join your followers, they will still have noticed you, and might remember your product in the future. So Promoted Accounts is a mix of pro-active advertising, where people come to your Twitter feed, and subtle advertising, where people don't look at the account, but have still been exposed to your brand colors and your existence.

Evidence suggests that Promoted Accounts appeal to users, and this means that they are more likely to be receptive to your Tweets in the future. The number of people encouraged to become followers will greatly exceed the number who will be prepared to stay once they have read a few Tweets or joined in with conversations, but if the Promoted Account attracts even 10% more long-term followers to your page, then you will have gained enormously.

In addition, as noted above, the promotional effects mean that even if you don't gain any direct followers from the Promotion, you will still have raised awareness of your business.

Using Promoted Accounts

For first-time users of Promoted accounts, it is important to be careful about balancing out enthusiasm for the new promotional systems with good, old-fashioned marketing techniques. Remember that the main purpose of using any promotion is to drive traffic to a website, or to encouraging promotions. Beginners should therefore concentrate upon creating good-quality Tweets, and limit the number of obvious product promotions until the new followers are comfortable. It is important to remember that it is not short-term followers that count, but those who stay for the longer term.

Businesses who have a lot of experience in Twitter might be able to generate more benefits from their promotions by timing a Promoted Account session with particular Tweets, perhaps selling a new product, running a competition, or anything else which is likely to bring in more people to your main website. Promoted Accounts can be used as time-specific events to coincide with specific drives, encouraging your followers to connect more with your business, or the launch of a new service which you think could help specific groups of Twitter users.

Cost and Value

The biggest note of caution to sound with Promoted Accounts is the cost. The promotions are charged at Cost Per Follower (CPF), which is calculated between $2-$4 a time. This means that it can quickly start costing a lot of money to keep promoting yourself online, with the price for 3 months being somewhere close to $15,000. Others have reported spending more than $100 in 2 minutes using this method, so business users need to calculate how much they are prepared to spend, and how much they expect to get in return. Not working this out before you join the Promoted Account group can be costly.

If you want to pursue Promoted Accounts, you will have to consider the value. This is the number of followers you have gained as a direct result of the Promotions. This is not always easy to work out, as Twitter provide a selection of data for the amount of clicks and followers promotions receive. It is possible to view this benefit during 6-hour time spans, allowing you to calculate just how much your following has grown during a particular period.

When you are considering using Promoted Accounts to reach Twitter followers, whether it is a specific targeting or a more generalized outreach, businesses need to consider whether it is of real value to your company. If you need to be able to reach a specific audience for only a short amount of time, then the Promoted Accounts might be very valuable. These would be short-term goals which are gratified by gaining a number of followers who could leave within a week of joining. However, in addition to short-term followers, businesses will gain increased brand awareness, simply by appearing on users' account pages, and on the Twitter homepage. This could be of benefit to the general health of the company.

For longer-term goals, businesses users will need to be more experienced at bringing in Twitter followers, and ensuring that they stay. However, long-term use of Promoted Accounts can be very costly, meaning that users will have to invest heavily in the promotion, and will often have little left over for any other kind of marketing campaign. Longer-term campaigns might include bringing in specific followers in order to generate interest in a particular product, or as part of a wider promotional campaign.

The best answer for Twitter business users considering Promoted Accounts is to try it for a short burst – perhaps only 30 minutes or so. Using the value calculators, you will be able to work out exactly how many followers were generated during that period. With this information, it should be possible to design a strategy which will make the best use of your new followers. Those with less money to spend will need to work harder at keeping the few followers they generate, so they might be more interested in the long-term benefits such as increased awareness of the brand, and recognition of the company. For those with a specific goal in mind, and with longer-term aims, it will be necessary to invest more in the promotions.

Introduce a Business to Twitter with Promoted Tweets

Businesses have been joining Twitter in large numbers, hoping to increase their brand recognition and generate greater profits for their company. Although some larger companies are able to get themselves high-ranking follower numbers almost immediately, smaller businesses struggle to attract more than a handful of followers at once. Thanks to the new advertising promotions which Twitter has developed, smaller companies may now be able to generate more interest in their Twitter account, and enlarge their follower list. Promoted Tweets are one way to ensure that a business account reaches more viewers.

What are Promoted Tweets?

The idea of a Promoted Tweets is that they resemble ordinary Tweets on a feed. They might contain the same information as a regular Tweet from the business account's feed, or they could be directly promotional, encouraging viewers to click a link or visit a website. They behave exactly like ordinary Tweets, in that they can be shared, replied to and retweeted. However, unlike ordinary Tweets from an average account, Promoted Tweets can be found in prominent places. This includes:

- The Home Page – Promoted Tweets are visible when logging in to the Twitter homepage

- Timeline – the feed of the Twitter homepage will include Promoted Tweets, and some users may find them in their timeline, if Twitter thinks there is a relevance

- Promoted Trend Results – Users can see Promoted Tweets in these search results, and may also be visible to users when they click on Promoted Trends

- Official Mobile and Computer Clients – including links such as Twitter for iPhone or Android and Tweetdeck. Third Party clients will also sometimes have Promoted Tweets

- Enhanced Profiles – Companies linked to Twitter may have Promoted Tweets at the top of their Twitter feed

Usefulness of Promoted Tweets

There are several reasons why businesses should consider using Promoted Tweets as part of their campaigns. Firstly, businesses who have used these Tweets in the past have found that they increase followers and readers by around 50%. This is a significant increase, and they enable the businesses to reach out to a much wider audience, which will help to raise brand awareness not only among those who receive the Promoted Tweet, but among all of their followers and readers, too.

Secondly, Promoted Tweets are sent to users who may already have an interest in your brand, or in the products and services that you have to offer. This can mean that you are able to target specific audiences, increasing the chances that you will boost your long-term Twitter following. The range of Twitter also means that many people use it to find services and products which they are interested in, and this is therefore an ideal place to put Promoted Tweets.

Thirdly, timeline-specific Promoted Tweets help to ensure

that your current followers are not backed-up with promotional Tweets, but they do allow the followers of those already in your Feed to see these Tweets, and this means that you can extend your regular followers.

Lastly, Promoted Tweets are also able to target specific groups, such as Twitter users from a particular location, or those using iPhones, Android and Blackberry devices. This means that new businesses can easily promote their products and brands to specific groups, such as those who live near to them, or who are interested in particular services that the company offers.

Benefits and Disadvantages to Promoted Tweets

Like any other form of advertising, Promoted Tweets have both advantages and disadvantages. In order to better understand how these can help a business, it makes sense to look at these pros and cons from a business perspective.

Advantages:

- Increased interest in your Twitter feed. This is perhaps the most direct advantage to using Promoted Tweets, since you are likely to get more engaged followers, and users who are interested and actively using your products and brand. If you want to make sure that you take followers over to a business website, then you may want to increase the click-rate of Twitter users who are not directly following you, but are looking for your product (perhaps after seeing a Promoted Tweet).

- Increased Purchases. This is one of the main aims of a social networking site, and so it makes sense that Promoted Tweets can be linked to increasing sales. If you decide to take this route, then your brand will need to actively participate in creating more searches for your product, both online and through the Twitter hub.

• Increased Brand Awareness. In addition to promoting general interest in your product, there is also an enhancement of brand awareness. This is true regardless of whether viewers click through, or simply view the Tweet on their home page. Effective use of brand colors is a must.

Disadvantages:

• Resentment: perhaps the biggest disadvantage to Promoted Tweets is the annoyance and resentment which viewers can experience on seeing the adverts. Most social media users are very resistant to the idea of advertising, and this can either make them completely indifferent to the product, or even deliberately ignore the Promoted Tweet on the grounds of their annoyance.

• Lost to Some Viewers. Another disadvantage to these Tweets is that they can be blank screens for third-party users. For those working with Hootsuite or similar unofficial systems, Promoted Tweets are not visible. In addition, Twitter cannot calculate the effectiveness of these Tweets in third-party programs, so you will not know if you are wasting your time, or benefiting most from these audiences.

Using Promoted Tweets

If you want to use Promoted Tweets to encourage people to

visit an external website, or just want to encourage visitors to your Twitter account, then there are several steps that you can take. It makes sense to try and create Tweets which are sophisticated, without too much sales-talk or obviously marketing your business. In order to make sure that you generate real interest, you need to use Tweets with great content, that are able to provide readers with genuine information, opinions or discussion topics.

Another way to use Tweets more effectively is to create more than one Promoted Tweet. This means that you can spread topics over a wider area, and it will also mean that you can target different areas of your potential audience. Having more than one Tweet also allows you to generate more interest in your company, rather than just a single Tweet which disappears quickly. You can also use these Tweets to create a 'story' or 'set a scene' much like a TV advert. This is likely to create interest.

Using a specific hashtag in Promoted Tweets will help you to create a buzz around your product or your Twitter feed. If you are specifically promoting the launch of a new product, or want to introduce some new aspect of your company, then the Hashtag is a great way of doing so. If you have decided to use more than one Promoted Tweet, then the hashtag used should be common to them all, not just to one Tweet.

You should also make sure that you monitor your Promoted Tweets, including viewing Twitter's statistics, to make sure that you really are reaching your target, and can provide your company with new users. You should look at these statistics before you start using the Promoted Tweets, making sure that you understand every aspect of how these Tweets can improve your business. A little research now will ensure that you are not spending money without good effect.

Using Promotional Tweets Positively

As noted above, there are certain elements of Promotional Tweets which have positive connotations, including the fact that they engage viewers, and are targeted towards people who would already be receptive. The positive elements of these Tweets can actually be used to help create a greater interest in your product, as long as they are used wisely. Engaging posts which are relevant to your particular target group are the best Promotional Tweet, since they combine the purpose of bringing people to your Twitter feed, and also generate their own interest, aside form your promotion.

Businesses also need to remember that there are negative elements connected with these Tweets, one of which includes those who are hostile to advertisements. While you cannot deflect all of this hostility, at least some of it could be mellowed by creating interesting, engaging or informative Tweets which encourage discussion and conversation, rather than simply urging a viewer to click on a particular page. You can also help to deflect this hostility by using targeting which helps to generate interest.

Combining the Tweets to produce something which is both positive and designed to negate hostility is not easy. Businesses might choose to employ someone creative to write those Tweets, or perhaps spend several hours designing and testing the content of each Tweet. Remember that engaging and creative content is the best way to increase the profile of your business, and will make paying for Promoted Tweets worthwhile.

Getting Your Tweets to Fly - How to Successfully Promote Your Twitter Business Account

When Twitter was first introduced, any business that had any account was ahead of the curve. Companies put little thought into their Twitter marketing strategies – by posting consistently, they spread word of their business almost effortlessly. It was easy to get noticed during a time when so few business owners utilized the now popular website. These days, Twitter is awash with accounts – people flock to the social networking site to relay personal, business, profit, and nonprofit messages to each other and the rest of the world.

Each message or "tweet" is limited to 140 characters (though in some instances it has been known to extend up to 160) – this means that those using Twitter have only a very small amount of space to convey what they need to say. This character limit is both a blessing and a curse: many see the short space as limiting, but short and succinct messages are all the rage these days. You can think of tweets as public text messages – short, sweet, and to the point.

Why Twitter?

How does Twitter fit into your business model? By connecting you with customer worldwide, a Twitter account can let you project your image, communicate news and advancements, and drum up excitement for your brand and products. Just like a Facebook account, Twitter allows people to follow your company and keep abreast of anything you post. This sort of open communication with customers is something that business owners have wanted for decades, and it's not available to you, the business owner, free of charge!

Getting your Twitter account noticed, however, is the bigger issues. The real key to getting spotted in the modern-day crowding of Twitter is to successfully manage your material, your interactions with others, your cross-promotion, and your sharing techniques. Employing all of these methods, you too can join the ranks of businesses whose tweets fly high.

Content

You may have heard the adage before, but it bears repeating – content is king. Your written content is the foundation on which your Twitter account is built, and without it your Twitter won't be going anywhere. You can invest boatloads of time in promotion and sharing your Twitter account with the world, be connected with hundreds of thousands of customers, but if you never post anything it will all be for naught.

The one rule about content is that what you write needs to be valuable to your readers. Many people wonder how they can make what they write interesting, catchy, or intriguing... but overall, all your readers will worry about is whether or not your tweets offer value to them. Defining that value is, of course, the tricky part. Try to think from a customer's perspective – if you were them, why would you be interested in what you had to say?

Your content can be flexible, and often you'll want to try and locate other things – news, bits of information, or pieces of gossip – that will be of use/interest to your readers. This is where staying connected to the right news sources for your business is crucial. As a business owner, you are likely informed when it comes to area of your market that are booming, trending, or flopping... why not share some of that interesting info with your followers?

Additionally, you'll want to develop a voice for your content. Do you want to be funny? Lighthearted? Serious? Conversational? Informative? Take a look other popular Twitter accounts to get an idea of what their voice is like. When you develop an online voice, you will quickly attract customers and followers who enjoy reading material kept within that frame.

Whatever strategy you take with your written content, make sure that its frequency is high. Not too frequent – no one wants to see you tweet twenty times a day. If you are a business, however, you may need to post more frequently than you think. If your business has a Facebook account, you may be used to posting on a daily or semi-daily basis. Twitter, however, demands a lot more content from those with a dedicated account. You'll want to send tweets out anywhere from 5 to 10 times each day.

Customer and Interpersonal Communication

The second most important step to successfully promoting your business-based Twitter account is customer interaction. At the heart of Twitter is interaction – retweeting, replying to personal tweets, and conversations between people are what set this networking site on its own unique pedestal. While having a Facebook account can sometimes feel like owning an island that people come to visit, having a Twitter account is more akin to setting up a housing development on that island and inviting people to live there.

Customers aren't the only ones you'll want to reach out to. Start researching other Twitter accounts in order to find people you relate to, you can connect with, and who can help you branch out to new customers and followers. People that you are following are listed openly on your Twitter page

– this means the people you follow are a direct representation of your business. Make that list of people count! Don't let the list stagnate – go out and find someone new to follow as often as possible, preferably a few times each week.

Because of Twitter's reliance on interpersonal communication, it's crucial that your business account cash in on these relations. Whenever you post a new tweet, you want to be replying, retweeting, or starting up at least one new conversation. This generally means your total daily posted Twitter content will be around 10-20 posts – this may sound like a lot, but the short length of each post makes them easy to complete.

Cross-Promotion

Cross promoting is a fantastic way to gather interest in not only your Twitter account, but all of your other online material, including your social network connections. What is cross promotion? Cross promotion is the act of utilizing several social networking mediums (or other websites) in order to promote and increase traffic to your Twitter.

Here is a perfect example: Your Facebook account is booming, but you've only just launched your Twitter and it doesn't have much of a following yet. You can then use your Facebook to reference a tweet you just posted, providing a link to that tweet where people can go and check it out for themselves. Chances are fairly high that those people who enjoy your Facebook with also enjoy your Twitter content. Of course, you can do this with any website and not just social networking sites – posting your Twitter content on your business's personal website is also a good way of cross promoting. Be sure to utilize the power of cross promotion in order to heighten interest in your Twitter account.

Dedicated Sharing Techniques

Lastly, it's important to recognize just how important it is too readily share your Twitter account information with those you meet on a daily basis. This goes for those you meet online and in person – after all, real people are the ones who own Twitter accounts, and just because you aren't meeting them through a computer doesn't mean that they don't use them at all!

Ever think of adding your Twitter address to your business cards? It's become commonplace to add your email address to business cards, but a new trend is developing of adding your Twitter information as well. You may be surprised to hear about this trend, but don't avoid it simply because it's new – hoping on the bandwagon now may get you a ton of followers down the road, especially in comparison to those who keep their business cards simple.

Have a dedicated website for your business? Consider posting about the most recent Twitter update on your news page or on a side bar that can be seen from every page of your website. This borderlines between cross promotion and dedicated sharing, but the important aspect is that people will be driven to visit your Twitter more frequently if you share what you write wherever you can.

Whatever ways you approaching sharing your Twitter, make sure you are approaching people that matter. What this means is that you should never try to pick up on the "get followers quick" scams – buying into these will likely get you followers, but they will mostly be "dummy" accounts led by fictitious people. What you want are real people with real opinions and real interest in your business. Don't bother buffering your account with insincere Twitter followers when real followers are worth so much more!

Getting your Twitter account to soar among the eagles takes a good deal of time and effort, but no business venture is made without some investment. Invest in your business's Twitter account via generating valuable content, interacting with customers, connecting with new people, and promoting your account – you'll be glad you did when your tweets are flying high!

Twitter Promotion and How it Can Help Your Business to Soar

If you're among those business owners who are dipping their toes into the Twitter pool (or perhaps you're cannon balling in wholeheartedly), you'll know by now that the social networking site can offer a wealth of connections. From boosting your company's signal, to getting to rub elbows with customers and new business associates, Twitter can be a fantastic social source. Any business owner should be tripping over themselves to create or improve their Twitter presence.

What's the next step for a savvy business owner like you? Promoting your tweets! Tweet promotion is still a fairly new concept, but with big name companies hoping on board straight away, smaller companies (and even those owning personal accounts) are now stepping up to bat. These tweets have been used for a myriad of purposes – from giveaways, questions, solicitations, and even complaints, promoted tweets have the power to shape what the online populace is seeing and thinking about.

If you're up for more people seeing your tweets, or would like to add the option of promoted tweets to your promotion model, there are a few things you'll need to know. You'll want to know how these promoted tweets work, when to use them, and what to include in these powerful messages.

What are Promoted Tweets?

Simply put, promoted tweets are messages that will appear in Twitter's search first – they'll be at the very top of the list, so they'll be seen by everyone who looks for that topic or any keywords or hashtags in the tweet. Companies and

167

businesses aren't the only ones who can utilize these specially promoted tweets – anyone who can afford the cost of the promotion can have their tweet pulled to the top of the list.

Twitter's promoted tweets have been compared to Google's Adsense model in the way that it gears content. Both models attempt to only send material towards those that are most likely to be interested in it, and both you a familiarly shaded background to denote which search results are sponsored and which aren't.

An example – you search for "party" on Twitter, looking to see what tweets show up. The first handful of tweets may have a slightly yellowish background color, and are most likely companies mentioning parties in their tweets. One retailer mentions how they are throwing an anniversary party for their company and hosting a giveaway of some products, while another company explains how they are a premier party supply chain. Yet another tweet is promoted to explain that a wealthy movie star is hosting his own personal party in celebration of a movie release. Below these promoted tweets will be popular tweets that are not promoted, most likely from personal accounts.

You can think of promoted tweets as a boost to organic sharing – you know that the tweet will be popular when enough people see it, the key is simply to get it seen by enough people. These tweets are available to those using conventional computers as well as those who tweet from their mobile devices, so your business tweets can be viewed by even more potential customers.

How to Promote Your Tweets

In order to actually promote a tweet, you'll need to first sign up with Twitter Ads. (This name might sound familiar: that could be because Google has a very similarly named site, named Google Ads.) Once you sign up, Twitter Ads leads you through the process step-by-step, judging what content you want to be seen, where you want it to be seen, and by whom.

The cost of tweet promotion is a flexible thing, as it is offering by a CPE basis – Cost Per Engagement. This means you only pay for the amount of times that someone checks out your tweet.

Twitter Ads lets you tweak, hone, and finalize your particular settings and preferences for who gets to see your tweet and where it will appear. The tweet can be set to appear in relevant search results, searches for promoted trends, home timelines, promoted pages, and even third-party clients.

How to Get the Most Out of Your Promotions

The most important part of promoting your tweets is not the promotion, but the tweet itself. The content, quality, and value of that tweet will affect how well the public receives it. There are four questions you will want to address before going ahead with your promotion.

- **What types of content should you promote?** We've established that promoted tweets are a powerful tool, but it should not be used for every tweet you post. Think of promoted tweets as the "secret weapon" of your Twitter marketing campaign – you certainly wouldn't pull it out at every chance you can, or it would lose its power and effectiveness quickly. In the case of promoted tweets, the cost of promoting every tweet would also take a big chunk out of your wallet. In general, aim to only promote tweets that have some real value to those outside of your current fan base. Remember that these tweets will be seen by everyone, and will represent you and your business – make whatever you say worthwhile, interesting, or at the very least entertaining.

The best time to promote a tweet is when you have a large event, big news, a giveaway or content, or a new product release. These things are what will intrigue people the most, and can get them clicking on your tweet more readily.

• **How can you aim your content efficiently?** Just like any form of marketing, promotional material on Twitter needs to be aimed properly in order to be effective. If you own your business, chances are you've done some sort developing a niche market, discovering your audience, and figuring out how to gear your marketing strategy toward the most fertile and willing crowd of customers. You'll need to use everything you've learned thus far about your company's audience in how you aim your promotional tweets.

Be aware that content that is not properly aimed can annoy those who see it, and thus affect your company in a negative way rather than a positive one. Twitter users can't opt out of seeing these promoted tweets either. If the particular tweet doesn't apply to them, the best they can do is dismiss it and hope that a similar tweet does that crop up again.

• **How can you use keywords to enrich your tweets?** Keywords are exactly as they sound – words that are key to your business. It's important that you define a list of these keywords, as they will be different for each company. If you run a bakery, some of your keywords may be "bakery", "bake", "cakes", muffins", "flour", "homemade", and more.

Using these keywords in your tweets can ensure that people searching for those words will be sent to your tweet. This means you should work to try and include a handful of these keywords in any tweet that your promote – it will increase clicks, traffic, and interest in your topic. Be sure, however, that the keywords you choose are good ones – what sort of words (that can be associated with your business/product) would make you click on a tweet?

- **How can you use hashtags correctly?**
Hashtags can be a powerful tool to connecting thousands of people up to your tweet, if used correctly. Hashtags are essentially a tag that can be searched through by anyone. Say, for example, you write a tweet about your favorite muffin recipe: "I love my new muffin recipe. So tasty!" That tweet can be seen by anyone who is following you. However, if you instead put: "I love my new #muffin recipe. So #tasty!" Anyone using or following the #muffin or #tasty hashtags will be able to see your tweet. Pay attention to what hashtags are currently trending, as that will boost your viewers. If you can't think of any hashtags to include in your tweets, refer back to your keywords – they often make fantastic hashtags.

An example of a useful hashtag would be ones such as #coupon #deal or #bargain. People search these tags on a daily basis to see if they can find great deals – if you're offering such a deal, sale, or bargain, people will be thankful that you have utilized the proper hashtag and alerted them to the sale!

Twitter Ads has even more information about promoted tweets, outlining the ins and outs of its promoted tweet program. If you're interested in digging a bit deeper into how Twitter plans to drive traffic to your tweet, you might want to check in with their available information before getting started.

Swimming through the thousands of tweets can feel overwhelming, especially if you're trying to breach the surface and get some real air time. Driving your business forward via Twitter can be a challenge, but by utilizing the power of promoted tweets you could see a boost in your customer base and interest in a matter of a few days.

Trending Tweets - Why Your Business Should Seek to Reach the Top

What is a Trending Topic on Twitter?

If you've ever been on Twitter, chances are you've seen the trending topics. They are often listed in plain sight on the left hand side of the page. They consist of a list of topics based on popularity, location in the world, and more. These topics listed are keywords and/or hashtags that are trending – their popularity has grown immensely, and/or they are words that are being used with some frequency among Twitter users. You'll usually see some mentions of holidays, politics, and world news make their way on to the list of trends.

As a business owner, this list can be a goldmine. Your Twitter business account can easily utilize these trending topics in the tweets you post and therefore gain a few more potential followers. But what if you wanted to start your own trend? How could you start? What do you need to know about how to launch that trend into the public's eye and foster organic sharing? There are some real pros and cons to promoting your own trend, but the pros can far outweigh the cons as long as you proceed with a keen eye and a level head.

Promoting a Trend – The Benefits

Being able to get your own unique idea for a trend out into the masses is a fantastic opportunity. When promoting a trend, your business will be seen by thousands (if not more) pairs of eyes. Not every person who sees the trend will check out your page, and not every person who checks out (and maybe even enjoys) your page will tweet your trending topic, but the amount of people who do will still be significantly higher than if you did not promoted a trend at all.

Twitter has proven to be a great platform to garner social interest – it isn't built specifically form marketing, which is why conventional users enjoy it and why businesses can benefit from it. For once, businesses are given a chance not to always be explaining why their products are the best. The best Twitter business pages are filled with personal stories, interesting conversations, and lighthearted humor. When you promote a trend, you are promoting your business in a personable, relatable way that people will appreciate and enjoy.

The Downside of Promoting a Trend

When you promote a trend, you are essentially giving the public free reign to use that topic in whatever way they please. Sadly, due to the nature of the internet, this often goes horribly wrong. There have been many promoted trends that have horror stories attached – even (or especially) big name companies has seen their trends twisted and distorted. There are also many trends that simply aren't picked up by the populace – they find them uninteresting, hard to tweet about, or not engaging enough.

A big show-stopper for many people is the price tag – promoting a trend now costs $200,000 a day. When Twitter originally launched their trend promoting campaign, the cost was significantly less: only $80,000 a day. With the phenomenal growth Twitter has seen in the past few years, it's easy to see why they are charging more – a trend on Twitter is seen by far more people now than it was in 2010 when the program was introduced. Smaller organizations or business owners may cringe at the large price, but you pay for what you get: being seen by the majority of Twitter's users is no small advertisement scheme.

The Bottom Line – Will You Benefit from Promoting a Trend?

The real question for business owners is that of dollars and cents – how effectively does a promoted trend boost your signal? Will people even notice your business, or will they simply share the trending keyword or hashtag for a day or two and then forget about you? With the large investment needed to promote a trend, there is good reason to ask a lot of questions about the usefulness for a business promoting a trend.

According to a recent study done by Twitter's Advertising Team, the results are positive for those who promoted a trend. They found that trend promotion generates an increase of brand advocacy – people speaking positively about a brand because they saw it trending recently. There was an average of over 150% increase in Twitter chatter about the companies promoting the trend. Lastly, the study found that the 24-hour window of the trending promotion didn't mean that folks only talked about it on one day – the brand focus and chatter would be anywhere from 20% to 70% more than the average chatter. That interest is nothing to sneeze at, and it's something many companies would be willing to spend the $200,000 to attain.

How to Successfully Aim Your Promoted Trend

There are a great deal of things that can go wrong when promoting a trend, but this doesn't make it any less valuable. If anything, it begs careful research, critical analysis, and clear planning before taking the steps to promote a trend.

When brainstorming your particular trending topic words, be sure to address your choices with the following factors in mind.

- Your trend should be intriguing. While it's not a complete requirement, you should try to pick a trend keyword that will draw people in and intrigue them, making them wonder what you're all about. Here's an example – a company that sells a waterproof spray-on protective coating for clothing wants to promote a trend. They decide to go with #spilleditallovermyself and ask that people share stories about times where they could have used a protective coating like the one that they sell. This, of course, leads to people sharing hilarious stories about times where they spilled drinks, embarrassed themselves, or otherwise made a mess. While this example may be a little over the top, the #spilleditallovermyself hashtag is intriguing, and makes you want to go check out what it's all about.

- The trend needs to be exciting. Twitter users should be excited to be a part of your trend – it should be one of the first things they want to tweet about when they log on for the day. The best way to come up with an exciting trend is to brainstorm what you yourself would find interesting. Try researching previous popular promoted trends to see why they succeeded, and what made them so exciting to Twitter users. Excited people enjoy spreading that excitement, and it will usually spread from your trend to your business page. Excited people also enjoy sharing their excitement with friends, family, and anyone they might run into – this means word of mouth, both digitally and physically.

- It's highly important for you to make the trend engaging. There is one thing that ties excitement and intrigue together, and that's pure engagement. When you've engaged your audience, they'll be willing to open their arms to your business – a level of trust will have been solidified if you manage to engross your audience in a positive manner. Generally this is done by allowing the trend to require direct and personal interaction from users who tweet about the trend. An example of this would be #mymostembaressingstory. It's simple enough, but users will get a real kick out of posting tweets about their most memorable embarrassing moment. You'll need to come up with an engaging trend that also ties in directly to your business – that, of course, is the tricky part. When a trend has both elements, it shines and grows in popularity.

- Above all, make sure the trend is effective. What are you seeking to achieve with this trend? What would you like people to say when they post about it in their tweets? Would you like to getting opinions about a new product? Analyze reactions to your company? See how the mind of your customers tick? Or would you simply like more people to be aware of your business and develop some brand loyalty? Whatever your goal is, make sure that your promoted trend works to achieve that goal. Some trends that are promoted hang out in space, achieving little or nothing. The trend may even be a good trend that gains a lot of popularity and usage, but if it doesn't tie back to the business or a business goal, there is little reason to make such a huge investment.

Promoting a trend successfully takes a good deal of both business and social media knowledge – a savvy Twitter user will know what is appropriate for a trending topic, while a businessman will know how to tie the engagement, excitement, and intrigue back into their product. Promoting a trend can have massive positive influence on your business, but only if utilized properly – before making the jump, make sure to invest not only money, but a great deal of time and forethought.

Why Promoted Trends Can Help Businesses to Improve their Twitter Ranking

Using a Promoted Trend to generate interest in a business is a new innovation by the people behind Twitter, and is proving to be very popular with companies who were in the middle-ranking stream of Twitter users. Promoted Trends are also a good way of generating more than just mild interest in a product, brand or new idea within the business itself, as it can raise awareness of all of these areas, and will also encourage people who would not otherwise have seen your Twitter account to become followers. This is very important for the on-going use of Twitter as a business tool, and will also mean that you can engage with the general public in ways that you might not have expected otherwise.

What are Promoted Trends?

Business users who are new to Twitter might not really understand what a Trend is, and would also not know what a Promoted Trend is. In order to use it as a way to create more interest for your company among targeted sections of the Twitter community, it is important to know how Trends are used in Twitter, and what they mean to the average user.

Trends on Twitter are created by the use of hashtags. These are phrases or keywords which appear at the end of a Tweet, and are begun with the symbol #, sometimes called the 'pound sign'. This hashtag creates a link which connects all of the Tweets containing the keyword or phrase, and Twitter then 'counts' these, or assesses them using a computer algorithm. The hashtags which appear most frequently are designated as 'Trends', and the hashtag is considered to be Trending. This Trend can go up or down, depending upon how many users add the keywords to their

Tweets during the course of 24 hours. The algorithm constantly updates the Trends, so what was important yesterday might not even feature on the list today.

All of the keywords which are Trending are found on the Twitter homepage, but they can also be located using 'Discover', or through active searches on the Twitter site. It is also possible to view Trends beyond those which Twitter thinks you might like to see, or specify locations or advanced searches.

Promoted Trends were designed to be used in connection with the Promoted Tweets feature, but have grown independently, and are now a completely separate feature of Promoted items on Twitter. In Promoted Trends, users are shown trends which have been featured by companies, and are specific to that user in terms of content, relationship to interests, or are connected to previous Trends that the user followed. Promoted Trends are bought by businesses to increase their visibility among the general population of Twitter users, and are clearly labeled as 'Promoted' on the Trends list. However, just like an ordinary Trend, the viewer can click on them to see the hashtag and keywords, and followers can also use the hashtag to increase interest in the company they are following.

Promoted Tweets and Promoted Trends

Business users are often unsure whether to use Promoted Tweets or Promoted Trends as the basis for a Twitter campaign. This can be a very difficult decision, as both have positive and negative values connected with them. In fact, it is sometimes hard to work out exactly where the Tweets begin and the Trends end. They both serve the same purpose, in that they encourage users to go to a Twitter account, and view the timeline, and perhaps follow the user.

They can also have a similar impact on the amount of follow-on Tweets, conversations and re-tweets that are used after a Promotional campaign.

Using Promoted Tweets requires a lot more effort, particularly as Businesses usually pay for more than one promotion at a time. They are also not connected to Trends, so they are generally less popular, and less likely to create a Trend when just used by themselves. On the other hand, they are more affordable, and will generate some level of interest.

Using Promoted Trends means concentrating the attention on the hashtags you are creating, but if used correctly, they can be much more effective in generating Tweets about your company, and inspiring conversation. While they do cost more than just Promoted Tweets, the Trend is more effective, and in that sense more valuable than Tweets alone.

Using Promoted Trends

In order to generate interest in your Twitter feed, and by extension in your brand, it is important to have a plan before you sign up to Promoted Trends. Consider what you are hoping for when you start using trends. Make a list of important strategies occurring over the next few months, and then make a list of how often you intend to Tweet. Combining these on a computer calendar will help you to visualize important patterns of promotions and Tweets, and will also tell you when products will need to be launched. By working out when your promotions and Tweets will come together most strongly, you can then set out a timeline for creating Promoted Trends, which will lead back to those Tweets, and eventually to the promotion.

Another important thing to consider when creating your

Trends is to generate interest outside of the hashtags. This means putting effort into the appearance of your Twitter account, and also ensuring that visitors are able to see interesting colors, see visuals, graphs and other illustrations on your Tweets, and that all of your Tweets are short and to the point. Visitors will not want to view long stories spread over several Tweets. Instead, keep each separate message unique.

In addition, it also makes sense for you to try and get the most from your viewers by paying attention to feedback. All too often, Twitter business users simply ignore the feedback from the general public, perhaps not interested in anyone who is not working in the industry, or perhaps not realizing how important feedback can be. Instead, if anyone messages you with information about your Promoted Trends, perhaps informing you that one hashtag is not working, or looks awkward compared to the other you are using on your timeline, then it makes sense to listen to that advice, and try and correct your mistakes. Make sure to talk to the message-sender about the information they provided, and thank them.

Lastly, it is important to remember that, while both Trends and Tweets can be bought and used as promotions, you should not be happy to let your efforts rest there. Instead, you should always try to keep the momentum flowing by initiating a secondary campaign of ordinary Tweets and hashtags, which will not all be connected with your business.

Promoted Trends: Costs and Value

The reason that more businesses don't use Promoted Trends is the high cost of these placements. If you want to get into the Trending box, you can expect to pay somewhere around $200,000 a day. This can be a big expense to most small businesses, and in fact it has meant that many companies avoid using this method of self-promotion. However, there are also good reasons for choosing Promoted Trends, and this is in the value of the hashtag. When that promotion appears in the box, it can generate over 1,000 Tweets every hour, and more interesting Tweets can be re-Tweeted, discussed and replied to at nearly 150 Tweets per hour. Even if your company lands somewhere in the middle of this, then the Promoted Tweets should earn their money back by generating so much interest in the business.

In order to understand fully how well you have done, you need to consider buying a Hashtag analytics program which will help you to discover how the Hashtag is trending, how many impressions have been generated each day, and the pattern of its Trending over a 24 hour period. This can be an expensive tool, depending on how many hashtags you are currently using to promote the business, but it can help you to increase the use of certain Promoted Trends, and to remove others which have not proven their worth.

Are Promoted Trends Worth It?

Businesses always want to know the value and worth of something before they try it, and Promoted Trends are no different. Users should always be aware that some viewers will consider that promotions on Twitter are misplaced, and so you could lose their interest for good. However, you are also likely to reach a much wider audience than if you simply stuck to using Twitter as a member of the general public, without one eye on the business element. This is a fine balancing act, but one which a business could do well to consider.

In order to make sure that your followers are not alienated by

Promoted Trends, it is a good idea to use Hashtags which are already trending among your community. These trends, if relevant to your promotion, or in any way connected to your business, can provide the key to creating a link between everyday trends, and Promoted Trends designed to encourage others to visit your Twitter account.

Summing Up

Well, you've made it this far and I appreciate the effort you have made. My sincere hope is that you have found something of value in each of the chapters and that you will be moved to improve your approach to Twitter and harvest great value in doing so.

Before finishing up, I would like to revisit a couple of the ideas that ran throughout the book. They are, by far, the most important and can be the hardest to master. None of them involve technology or applications. They all focus on how you relate to the people you come in contact with – how you relate to them.

• Always remember that Twitter is, at its very core, a social media. That means that the serious users – the ones you are most looking to engage with - expect you to 'be social'. Develop and then refine the ability to 'chat' in a way that is supportive, respectful and contributes to the experience of your followers and those you follow.

• Remember that content is king in Twitter. An important part of your presence – your branding – is the quality of your Tweets. You want to be seen as a person worth paying attention to. You want followers who have singled you out from among the 'shallow water sailors' as someone they want to associate with.

• Remember that your brand is influenced by those who you associate with and those who choose to associate with you. Savvy Twitter users will check out both as they decide whether you are worth their time and attention.

• Remember that users who simply bleat one Tweet after another are quickly dismissed. Conversations are the holy grail of Twitter. The more you engage with people, the stronger your brand will be and the more interested they will be in what you have to say.

• Remember that Twitter and the establishment of your brand is a long-distance journey. It's going to take time to develop the kinds of relationships that will help you achieve your goals.

• Remember to keep confusion to a minimum by not introducing irrelevancies into your Tweets. The best brands are tightly focuses.

- And finally, remember that Twitter is best used with a light touch. It is important to have a bit of fun – to enjoy your time on the platform. A complement, a friendly response, a constructive addition to someone's Tweet will go a long way towards making you a valuable and valued member of the Twitterverse.

Dr. Earl R. Smith II
DrSmith@Dr-Smith.com
www.Dr-Smith.com
Washington, DC
June 2014

My hope is that you have found this book useful. If you are so inclined, please leave a review. Reviews are way to tell the world what you thought of Twitter Super-Charged and it would be of great help to me. Thanks for buying the book and I look forward to hearing any comments or suggestions for its improvement that you might have.